SINGAPORE AND MALAYSIA

Varieties of English Around the World

General Editor:

Manfred Görlach
Anglistisches Seminar der Universität
Kettengasse 12
D-6900 HEIDELBERG
Germany

TEXT SERIES
Volume 4

John Platt, Heidi Weber and Mian Lian Ho
Singapore and Malaysia

SINGAPORE AND MALAYSIA

by

John Platt, Heidi Weber and Mian Lian Ho
Monash University,
Clayton, Australia

JOHN BENJAMINS PUBLISHING COMPANY
AMSTERDAM/PHILADELPHIA

1983

ACKNOWLEDGEMENTS

We are grateful to the following for permission to reproduce copy-right material:

Times Periodicals Pte Ltd for an excerpt from This Singapore 1975, Professor Wang Gungwu and Educational Publications Bureau Pte Ltd for the poem 'Ahmad' by Wang Gungwu in The Flowering Tree, 1970. Woodrose Publications Private Limited for excerpts from the poems 'Big Spender' by Ernest Lim and 'Eden 22' by Mervin Mirapuri in Singapore Writing, 1977, Oxford University Press (Kuala Lumpur) for excerpts from the play 'A Tiger is Loose in our Community' by Edward Dorall in New Drama One, 1972, Heinemann Educational Books (Asia) Ltd for an excerpt from the poem 'a singapura sequence' by Muhammad Haji Salleh in Second Tongue, 1976, excerpts from the short story 'Everything's Arranged' by Siew Yue Millingley in 22 Malaysian Stories, 1968, excerpts from the short stories 'The Taximan's Story' and 'The Teacher' by Catherine Lim in Little Ironies - Stories of Singapore, 1978 and excerpts from the short story 'A.P. Velloo' by Catherine Lim in Or Else, the Lightning God and Other Stories, 1980, Kirpal Singh for excerpts from the play 'One Year Back Home' in Singa 2, 1981, an excerpt from the short story 'PUB Bills' by Ho Khek Fong in Singa 3, 1981, and the short story 'Little Sister Writes Home' by Kirpal Singh in The Interview and Other Stories, 1983.

Thanks are due to those many Singaporeans and Malaysians who allowed us to interview them, those Singapore students who wrote impromptu compositions for us and to their parents who gave us per-mission to use them.

Special thanks go to Ursula Kutschbach who typed the draft manu-script for us and to June Roder and Daniela Antas who worked patiently and intelligently to produce this final version.

Some of the texts are from interviews which were conducted in con-nection with research projects supported by Australian Research Grants Committee Grants A68/1601 and A77/15355 to J. T. Platt.

                                                    J.T.P.
                                                    H.W.
                                                    H.M.L.

CONTENTS

II Written English

A Compositions and notes

B From advertising leaflets etc.

C From newspapers

III Local Media Comments on Singapore English

IV English in Literature (excerpts)

A Poetry

B Drama

C Prose

REFERENCES

INTRODUCTION

This volume is a collection of varieties of spoken and written English of Singpaore and Malaysia, including a range of spoken English transcribed from recordings, examples of informal writing, English in the press and English in literature. It will be seen that there is a very wide range, from a formal 'international' English to highly distinctive types spoken by those of lower educational and socio-economic status.

In order to understand the present status of English in the two nations and why English has developed as it has, it is necessary to view it in a historical and social perspective from the beginning of British colonial influence to the post-Second World War expansion in educational opportunity, national independence and, in the case of Malaysia, the introduction and implementation of a national language policy which has diminished but by no means eliminated the importance of English.

The earliest British colony on the Malay Peninsula or adjacent islands was Penang, which was established by Francis Light in 1786. Singapore was founded by Sir Stamford Raffles in 1819, and Malacca was taken over from the Dutch in 1824. The two island possessions, Penang and Singapore, the town of Malacca along with some surrounding country and the island of Labuan off the coast of Borneo later became the British Crown Colony of the Straits Settlements.

The British gradually extended their sphere of influence over the Malay Peninsula and by 1896 the four Malay States of Perak, Selangor, Pahang and Negri Sembilan were formed into a federation, the Federated Malay States, each state having a British Resident to advise the Sultan. A British administrative organization developed, not only for each state but for the whole Federation, with Kuala Lumpur as the capital. By 1914, British influence had extended to the remaining five states which, however, did not join the Federation. In general, the importance of English was greatest in the Straits Settlements of Singapore, Penang and Malacca and least in the Unfederated Malay States - with the exception of Johore Bahru, the capital of Johore state, which is very close to Singapore.

Even when the British first arrived, the population in some areas was far from homogeneous. Apart from the Malays and small groups of aboriginal people, there were already Chinese engaged in tin mining and trading, and some Indian merchants. In Malacca, which had been a Portuguese and then a Dutch colony, there was a group of mixed ethnic background speaking a Portuguese-based creole and a sizeable group descended from earlier Chinese immigrants who had married Malay women. These 'Straits-born Chinese' (known also as Peranakan or Baba Chinese) spoke a Malay-based creole. Later on, the Straits-born Chinese were particularly interested in having their children educated at English-medium schools.

With the expansion in tin mining and the development of rubber plantations, large numbers of immigrants from Southern China and Southern India arrived in the later 19th and early 20th centuries.

By 1911, the ethnic distribution in the Federated Malay States and Singapore was as follows (raw figures from Handbook to British Malaya, 1926):

Federated Malay States

Europeans	Eurasians	Malays	Chinese	Indians	Others
3,284	2,649	420,840	433,244	172,465	4,517
0.32%	0.26%	40.58%	41.78%	16.63%	0.44%

Singapore

Europeans	Eurasians	Malays	Chinese	Indians	Others
7,368	8,072	240,206	369,843	82,055	6,525
1.03%	1.13%	22.64%	51.79%	11.49%	0.91%

Because of the multi-ethnic situation, a complex network of language use developed. Among the Chinese, there were a number of so-called 'dialects' spoken, some of these not being mutually intelligible. The predominant group in the Straits Settlements was Hokkien speaking and they are still the main Chinese group in Penang, Malacca and Singapore. In the tin mining regions of Selangor and Perak the Cantonese were and still are the main Chinese group. The other main groups are Teochew, Hakka (Kheh) and Hainanese. In the north and south of the Malay Peninsula, including Penang, Malacca and Singapore, Hokkien became the lingua franca among the Chinese, whilst in the central region: Selangor, the southern part of Perak, and Pahang, Cantonese fulfilled the same function.

Among the Indians, the Tamils were predominant but other Dravidian languages, e.g. Malayalam and Telugu, were spoken as well as Northern Indian languages such as Punjabi, Sindhi and Bengali.

The overall inter-group lingua franca was a pidginized form of Malay, Bazaar Malay (Bahasa Pasar) and this is still widely used among older people in inter-ethnic communication if one at least of the participants has had little or no education in an English-medium school.

At first, the use of English was very restricted. It was the language of the British administration and British employees in private business. It was also the language for legal matters in the Straits Settlements and later for many areas of justice in the Malay States. Interpreters were used where necessary.

As Britain had established its presence earlier in India, there were already English-speaking Indians at the time when the Straits Settlements were being established, and some of these came to the Straits Settlements and Malaya to work as clerks in government and private offices. When schools teaching through the medium of English were established, numbers of Indians found employment as teachers. These Indian teachers certainly had an influence on the type of English which developed in Singapore and Malaya. There are similarities in lexical and syntactic usage between Singapore-Malaysian English and Indian English, although there are also considerable differences as well, and phonically they seem to be very distinct.

As has already been stated elsewhere (Platt 1976, 1977, Platt & Weber 1980) it was through the education system, in its widest sense,

that Singapore-Malayan English developed.   There was very little Pidgin
English spoken in the region as Bazaar Malay was used as the main lingua
franca and it was necessary for Europeans to acquire at least a basic
competence in it.

A few schools teaching through the medium of English were established in the early 19th century in the Straits Settlements of Penang,
Singapore and Malacca.   Gradually more schools were opened not only in
the Straits Settlements but also in the Malay States.   These were
government schools or schools run by church missions.   Church schools
eventually received government financial support and an inspection system
was established.

Until after the Second World War, most of the students attending
these schools were the sons (and later the daughters) of the more pros-
perous Chinese and Indians, who realized the advantages of an English-
medium education, although there were, of course, many poorer parents
who made considerable financial sacrifices to give their children such an
education.   In general, the Malays lived in rural areas, and most Malay
children attending school went to Malay vernacular schools.   However,
there were some Malay sons of the aristocracy who attended English-medium
schools.

Whatever may have been the attitudes of non-Europeans to British
colonial policy or to European culture, it was obvious to many of them
that English-medium education had many material advantages and the number
of students at English-medium schools gradually increased so that by 1937
the total enrolment in the Federated Malay States was 17,161 (Loh 1975)
and in Singapore, the enrolment in 1941 was 27,000 (Doraisamy 1969).

In such multilingual societies as Malaya and Singapore, it became
apparent that there were other benefits accruing to those with some competence in English, not the least of which was the ability to communicate
with English-medium educated persons of other ethnic and language backgrounds.   Thus it was possible for Chinese to communicate with Tamils on
topics for which they would not have had the lexical range in Bazaar
Malay, and it became possible for Chinese of different dialect backgrounds
to converse in something other than a basic or 'reduced' form of the
dominant Chinese dialect.   English was the language of Western science
and technology and a knowledge of it was the key to understanding these,
as well as Western economics, political science, law, medicine and so on.
English, although an exoglossic language and the language of the colonial
rulers, was a unifying force in that it was becoming a lingua franca of
the more elite sections of society.

Because children were using English in natural communication
situations whilst still in quite early stages of acquisition - some of
them even acquiring some competence in it before school years from elder
siblings - a type of English developed which was strongly influenced by
the background languages, particularly the Chinese dialects and Malay.
Although students might go on to the acquisition of something closer to
a prescriptive 'Standard British English', they would revert in informal
situations to the stages of English they had acquired earlier.   Thus a
whole continuum developed, somewhat similar to what has been described
for post-creole continuum situations such as those in Jamaica (De Camp
1971) and Guyana (Bickerton 1975).   However, whereas a post-creole
continuum arises when members of a creole-speaking community have dif-
fering degrees of access to education in the superordinate 'standard'

language, a situation such as that in Singapore and Malaya arose mainly
through the acquisition of English by speakers of other languages
through the educational system and the use of English in natural,
meaningful situations by the learners themselves with others at various
stages in the acquisition process.   (cf Platt 1978, etc.)

Singapore received internal self-government in 1959 and later joined
Malaya, Sabah (North Borneo) and Sarawak to form the nation of Malaysia.
In 1965, Singapore separated from Malaysia but remained within the
British Commonwealth.   As Singapore and Malaya/Malaysia have, for most
of the post-war period, been separate nations with separate educational
and language policies, the position of English within the two nations can
best be considered separately.

Singapore

In 1947, the enrolment in English-medium schools was 29,095 as compared
with 53,478 in Chinese-, 6,464 in Malay- and 919 in Tamil-medium schools.
Therefore about 32% of students were enrolled in English-medium schools.
By 1952, the English-medium enrolment had increased to 63,386, 43% of the
total school enrolment.   (Enrolment figures from Doraisamy 1969.)

In 1956, an All-Party Committee recommended a bilingual educational
policy, with the language of instruction being either English, Chinese
(Mandarin), Malay or Tamil.   If English was the medium of instruction,
then one of the other three would be the second language;   if one of the
other three was the language of instruction, then English would be the
second language.

The proportion of enrolments in English-medium schools or 'streams'
continued to increase, passing 50% in 1962, reaching 58.7% in 1967, 71.3%
in 1976 and 79.9% in 1979.

Early this century, a medical college was established and in 1929,
another tertiary institution, Raffles College, was opened, serving mainly
as a training institution for teachers in the higher grades at English-
medium schools.   Both of these institutions taught purely through the
medium of English.   After World War II, they became part of the University of Malaya (later University of Singapore).   Recently, the Chinese-
medium Nanyang University was amalgamated with the University of Singapore
to form the National University of Singapore, which teaches entirely
through the medium of English.

Singapore's population of nearly two and a half million (Census of
Population 1980) is made up of approximately 77% Chinese, 15% Malays, 6%
Indians and 2% other small groups.   Among older speakers of English,
there are usually quite noticeable phonetic differences according to the
language background of the speaker.   However, among younger English-
medium educated Singaporeans, the merger has progressed to such a degree
that it is often difficult to judge a person's ethnic background purely
from their spoken English.

English has continued to become more and more important as the
language of commerce, science and technology and has increased not only as
an inter-ethnic but also as an intra-ethnic means of communication.
There are two daily newspapers in English as well as a range of magazines,
there is a considerable amount of English language on the radio, and
English-language films are shown on television and in cinemas.   Of course,

the use of English increases as one moves down the age scale but almost
all Singaporeans use some other language(s) or Chinese dialect(s) in
certain situations, e.g. with older people, with hawkers, in Chinese and
Indian restaurants (as against the Western-type restaurants, coffee
houses and bars) and with those in the employment sphere such as unskilled
workers.

Recently, the Prime Minister, Mr Lee Kuan Yew, has spoken frequently
of the need for Singaporeans to retain their traditional cultural values.
He has also urged the Singapore Chinese to use Mandarin rather than the
dialects so that they would have one common variety of Chinese.
However, the government is fully aware that competence in English is
vital for this small commercial and industrial nation and there is
emphasis on the need to improve the overall standard of English.

Malaysia

In Malaysia, the position of English has changed since Malaya became an
independent nation in 1957 and Malay was declared the National Language.
As early as 1956 it was suggested by an Education Committee that Malay
should be a compulsory language in all schools and that a knowlege of it
be necessary for admission to government or government-aided secondary
schools.   Malay was to be introduced as a subject in all schools and
Malay-medium secondary schools were to be established.

In 1956, 61% of the total secondary school population were enrolled
in government-aided English-medium schools - as against 34.4% in Chinese-
medium, 4.1% in Malay-medium and 0.4% in Tamil-medium schools.   By 1964,
the English-medium percentage had increased to 84.4% and the Malay-medium
to 15.6%.   There were no more government-aided Chinese or Tamil-medium
secondary schools.   By 1967, the percentage enrolment at English-medium
secondary schools had decreased to 69.1% but the enrolment at Malay-medium
schools had increased to 30.1%.   The reason for this increase was that
more Malay-medium secondary schools had been established, particularly in
rural areas.   In 1970, the Ministry of Education announced a policy by
which English-medium schools would be gradually converted to Malay-medium,
with the changeover at first year level taking place in 1971 and a target
of complete conversion at primary and secondary levels in 1982.   English
would remain as a compulsory second language.

Obviously this policy has meant a very different status for English.
At one time, English-medium education and competence in English were pre-
requisites for entrance to the professions, the government clerical and
administrative services and many private businesses.   Now a similar competence in Malay is essential for government positions and for many
private businesses.   Malay is being introduced as the medium of
instruction for various university courses, but English will remain
important in many areas of study as essential texts are in English.

There has been a general policy of change from English to the
National Language - Bahasa Malaysia.   Street signs and road signs are in
Malay, shops are required to display signs in the Malay language more
prominently than in other languages, official forms are in Malay, and
correspondence from government departments is also in the National
Language.

However, there are still a considerable number of English-language
television programmes and English-language films.   English-language 'pop'
music is played on one of the radio networks, and there are four English

language newspapers in Peninsular Malaysia.

Whereas in Singapore there are more and more speakers for whom English is something between a 'first' and 'second' language, because it is used daily in natural communicative situations (cf Platt & Weber 1981), in Malaysia, English is becoming more a 'foreign' language as it is being used less and less in such situations. The Malaysian government is, however, well aware of the importance of English and is concerned to maintain or even improve standards and the position of English is likely to remain an important one because of its status as the dominant inter-national language.

Some Characteristics of Singapore/Malaysian English

It must be mentioned here that the typical English (SgE) is spoken by the English-medium educated sector of the community, particularly those who use it in everyday verbal interactions. Those who are educated in Chinese-medium schools, or who received a Malay- or Tamil-medium education would usually not speak SgE. The older population with this type of education would use their local languages or dialects and Bazaar Malay and younger Singaporeans who had English as a second language and not as the medium of instruction speak English more as a learner's language. Two examples of 'borderline cases' of SgE have been included in this volume (Texts 11 and 12).

Most of the examples from Malaysian English (MalE) in the text volume follow the pattern of SgE as far as range (basilectal to acrolectal) and characteristics are concerned. This type of Malaysian English, referred to by Platt and Weber (1980) as Malaysian English Type I, will, of course, be gradually disappearing as from now on the younger population will have a Malay-medium education with English as a second language. Type II (cf Platt & Weber 1980) used by those with a Malay-medium education, will be on the increase. For comparison, one sample of this type is included (Text 33). It must be understood that as Type II is closer to being a learner's language, it is not so easy to obtain longer uninterrupted samples of natural speech such as are obtainable for SgE and MalE Type I.

a.   Pronunciation

SgE and MalE vary from Standard British English in a number of ways. Some of the noticeable differences are:

(1)   Final consonants appear more frequently unreleased than they do in Standard British English. Often they appear as glottal stops.

(2)   Consonant clusters, particularly final and some medial clusters, are reduced, e.g.

> jus instead of just
>
> tol instead of told

(3)   Initial fricatives /θ/ and /ð/ are often realized in an affricated form, that is as [t̪] or [d̪] followed by friction, e.g.

> [t̪ˢɪŋ]   thing

or as [s̪] or [z̪], e.g.

> [z̪ɪs]   this

or as [t̪] or [d̪], e.g.

[d̪ə]   <u>the</u>

(4) There are differences in vowel quality, which can be noticed particularly in the realization of the diphthongs, which are shorter than in Standard British English and often realized as monophthongs, e.g.

<u>take</u> is realized as   [tɛʔ]

<u>so</u>   is realized as   [so]

<u>dare</u> is realized as   [dɛ.]

(5) Word stress in multisyllabic words is inclined to shift to a later syllable, e.g.

<u>educáted</u>   instead of <u>éducated</u>

<u>distribútor</u>   instead of <u>distríbutor</u>

<u>usuallý</u>   instead of <u>úsually</u>

(6) Unlike Standard British English which tends towards a stress-timed rhythm, SgE and MalE tend towards a syllable-timed rhythm. In a completely syllable-timed rhythm, all syllables, stressed or unstressed, would recur at equal intervals of time. In SgE and MalE the final syllable of a tone unit is often somewhat lengthened.

A noticeable feature of more colloquial style is the use of Chinese particles which take the place of intonational features occurring in Standard English to convey emphasis and emotional attitudes etc., e.g.

Don'(t) wan(t) lah

where <u>lah</u> acts as an emphatic marker.

b. Morphological and Syntactic Features

(1) Variable occurrence of the various forms of BE, particularly before predicate adjectives and to some extent before predicate nominals, <u>-ing</u> constructions, temporals and locatives, e.g.

This coffee house .... very cheap

My father .... taxi driver

(2) Variable past tense marking, e.g.

My mum, she come from China many years ago

(3) Variable marking of 3rd person singular present tense, e.g.

This radio sound good

(4) The use of the completive aspect marker <u>already</u>, e.g.

Eight years she work already

(She's been working for eight years)

(5) The use of the habitual aspect marker <u>use to</u>, e.g.

My mother, she use to go to the market

(My mother goes to the market)

(6)   The use of <u>would</u> for future events, where Standard British English would use <u>shall</u> or <u>will</u> or a present tense construction, e.g.

       I trust that you would expedite matters

       We hope this would meet your requirements

(7)   The use of the existential <u>got</u>, e.g.

       In China, where got people go to English school?

       (In China, where are there people who go to English-medium schools?)

(8)   Variable noun plural marking, e.g.

       I have three sister and two brother

(9)   Variable lack of definite and indefinite articles

       You have pen or not?

       He wen(t) to office already

(10)   Substitution of a demonstrative (particularly <u>this</u> and <u>these</u>) for a definite article or the use of a demonstrative where no demonstrative or article would be used in Standard British English, e.g.

       I like this geography

       You can take this number 11 to Changi

(11)   Variable lack of subject or object pronouns, e.g.

       (I) speak Cantonese also

       Sorry, we don't have (it)

(12)   The use of <u>one</u> to form an adjectival group, e.g.

       Don'(t) throw away.   This type still can use one.

       (This type or this thing is still usable)

(13)   Preposing of direct or indirect object for emphasis, e.g.

       This book we don'(t) have

       To my sister sometime(s) I spea(k) English

(14)   Pronoun copying. In these cases, the subject or object appears first as a noun and then as a pronoun. This type of construction is very frequent in SgE/MalE, e.g.

       My husband he always like to gamble

(15)   SgE and MalE use the invariable tag question <u>is it?</u> and <u>isn't it?</u>, e.g.

       He also don'(t) know, is it?

       (He doesn't know either, does he?)

       You never late before, isn'(t) it?

       (You've never been late before, have you?)

(16)   Co-ordination without <u>or</u> or <u>and</u>, e.g.

       It cost(s) six seven dollars

(17) Lack of <u>if</u> in subordinate constructions, e.g.

> Canno(t) do, we as(k) for the serviceman to come lah
>
> (If we can't do it, we ask for the serviceman to come)

For a more detailed discussion of these and other features of Singapore and Malaysian English see Platt and Weber 1980.

c. Lexicon

There are a number of interesting words and expressions in SgE/MalE which come from the background languages, e.g.

<u>tamby</u> (from Tamil) 'an odd-job man in an office'

<u>makan</u> (from Malay) 'food' (in Malay 'food' is <u>makanan</u>;   <u>makan</u> means 'to eat')

<u>botak</u> (from Malay) 'bald'

<u>towkay</u> (from Hokkien) 'a Chinese businessman'

<u>ang pow</u> (from Hokkien) 'a gift of money' (traditionally in a red packet 'ang pow')

There are a number of words and expressions which are used differently in SgE/MalE from Standard British English:

<u>send</u>	I will send you home (meaning: I'll take you home in my car)
<u>gostan</u>	(from English 'go astern') Workman to lorry driver, guiding him into a drive-way. Gostan, gostan!
<u>stay</u>	Where do you stay? (Where do you live?)
<u>last time</u>	Last time he smoke a lot; now no more already. (He used (formerly) to smoke a lot but he doesn't any more.)
<u>open</u>	Open the light (Put the light on)

Special SgE/MalE lexical items which appear in the texts have been glossed by footnotes.

For a more detailed discussion of SgE/MalE see Platt and Weber 1980.

Sociolectal range within Singapore-Malaysian English

As with other varieties of English, the speech and writing of Singaporeans and Malaysians vary according to many factors.   There is a variation in speech patterns according to the educational and socio-economic background of the speakers.   Those who have had a tertiary education and are in higher status occupations speak a type of SgE/MalE which is closest to Standard British English whereas those who have had only a few years of English-medium education and lower status occupations speak sub-varieties

of SgE/MalE which are farther away from Standard British English.   It
must be understood here that by MalE we are referring only to MalE Type I.
Strictly speaking, as with any speech variety, there are no clear-cut
divisions, but it is useful to divide SgE/MalE into various sub-varieties.
If one considers the whole of SgE/MalE as speech continua then the sub-
variety at the bottom of the continuum may be referred to as the basilect,
the sub-variety at the top of the continuum as the acrolect and the sub-
varieties in between as the mesolects.   In the arrangement of the texts,
we have made a division into those texts which fall more into the
basilectal range of the continuum and those which can be considered as
mesolectal or acrolectal.   Tables 1, 2 and 3 (adapted from Platt and
Weber, 1980:102-104) show some of the ways in which these lects differ
from one another.

As is the case with many developing varieties of English, SgE/MalE
has no fully developed stylistic range within each sociolectal range.
Therefore the educated Singaporean or Malaysian, when speaking English,
drops down to a more basilectal SgE/MalE and uses it as his or her
colloquial style in informal situations, e.g. with friends or within the
family.

A comparison between established and newly developing varieties
with regard to stylistic and social variation can be seen in Figure 1
from Platt and Weber 1980:112.

FIGURE 1   Stylistic and Social Variation in
            Established and Newly Developing Varieties

I Established Varieties   II Newly Developing Varieties
   (e.g. St BrE)   (e.g. SgE)

Speech Community   Speech Variety   Speech Community   Speech Variety
(social scale)   (sociolectal   (social scale)   (sociolectal
                         scale)   scale)

F = Formal, SF = Semi-formal, Coll = Colloquial, HS = Highest Sociolect,
LS = Lowest Sociolect.

Table 1 Syntactic Features

Syntactic Features

	Acrolect	Upper Mesolect	Lower Mesolect	Basilect
Verb				
Past tense marking	Occasional d/t deletion after consonant	Frequent d/t deletion after consonant; Some d/t deletion after vowel; Sometimes no vowel change	d/t after consonant nearly always deleted, often no vowel change; Some d deletion after vowel; Some -ed deletion after t and d	Frequent d deletion after vowel; Frequent -ed deletion after t and d
Third pers. sing. pres. tense marking	Nearly always marked	Frequently marked	Frequently unmarked	Nearly always unmarked
to be as copular and before V-ing	Some deletion pre-Adj	Occasional deletion particularly pre-Adj	More frequent deletion pre-Adj,	Occasional deletion in all positions
Aspect Markers				
already	*	Some use	Some use	Frequent use
use(d) to	*	Some use	Some use	Frequent use
usually	Some use	Some use	Frequent use	Frequent use
would	Some use	Used quite frequently	Used quite frequently	Infrequent use
Noun Phrase				
Noun plural marking	Nearly always marked	Occasionally not marked	Occasionally not marked	Frequently not marked
Article, definite (the)	Rarely omitted	Rarely omitted	Occasionally omitted	Occasionally omitted
indefinite (a/an)	Rarely omitted	Occasionally omitted	Occasionally omitted	Frequently omitted
Subject pronoun: other than it	Always used	Rarely omitted	Frequently omitted	Frequently omitted
it	Rarely omitted	Occasionally omitted	Frequently omitted	Very frequently omitted
Object pronoun	Used	Nearly always used	Occasionally omitted (with certain verbs)	Frequently omitted (with certain verbs)
Focusing Devices (including pronoun copying)	Occasionally used	Occasionally used	Used frequently	Used very frequently

* Naturally, *already* and <u>used</u> to occur in the spoken acrolect but they are not used as Aspect Markers in the same way as they are used in the basilect, for instance.

Table 2

Table 2 Phonetic Features

	Acrolect	Upper Mesolect	Lower Mesolect	Basilect
Final consonants				
3 consonant clusters	Occasional deletion of one	Frequent deletion of one	Frequent deletion of one	Frequent deletion of two
2 consonant clusters	Occasional deletion of one, particularly final stops	Occasional deletion of one	Frequent deletion of one	Frequent deletion of one, occasional deletion of two
1 consonant	Rare deletion or substitution	Occasional deletion, occasional substitution particularly of glottal stop for k and t	Occasional deletion, frequent substitution of glottal stop for k and t	Higher degree of deletion, nearly always substitution of glottal stop for k and t
Initial dental fricatives as in the, this, through	Frequent use of affricated form e.g. $[t^s]$	Frequent use of affricated form	Mainly use of affricated form, some stops, e.g. $[d]$	Some use of affricated form, frequent use of stops
Vowels	Shortening of long vowels, often with no change in vowel quality (or something approaching it) for all sub-varieties			
(ou)	Mostly use of $[ɔ]$			
(ei)	Frequent use of $[e^ˡ]$ some $[ɛ^ˡ]$	Frequent use of $[ɛ^ˡ]$ some $[ɛ:]$	Use of both $[ɛ^ˡ]$ and $[ɛ:]$	Frequent use of $[ɛ:]$ and $[ɛ]$
Stress	More even stress pattern than in many other varieties of English			
Syllable stress shift to later syllables	On a few occasions	Quite common	Quite common	Frequent
Sentence intonation	More even rhythm than in many other varieties of English, heavier stress in phrase and sentence final position			

Table 3 Lexical Features

x = very common in this lect.

	Acrolect	Upper Mesolect	Lower Mesolect	Basilect
Words and expressions from background languages	Occasionally used (part. in the media)	Frequently used	Frequently used	Frequently used
Tendency to participialize	To a lesser degree than the other sub-varieties	x	x	x
Tendency to abbreviate	x	x	x	x
Tendencies in lexical choice	To a lesser degree than in			

The Texts

The texts in this volume are divided into four main sections: I. Spoken English, II. Written English, III. Media Comments and IV. English in Literature.   Many of the spoken texts were obtained in interviews and are extracts from recordings made of some 300 Malaysians and Singaporeans between 1974 and 1982.   Some of the spoken English texts are conversations which involve speakers of Singapore or Malaysian English.

It must be emphasized that this selection of texts, whilst indicating characteristics of Singapore and Malaysian English, cannot be used for quantitative analysis of particular variables, e.g. Past Tense marking or copula occurrence as far larger samples would be needed. For analyses of variation in Singapore English, the reader is referred to various publications by Platt and by Platt and Weber listed under References.   However, the texts do illustrate a great many of the phonological, morpho-syntactic and lexical features which make Singapore-Malaysian English distinctive.

The texts in the section on Spoken English are divided into two sub-sections: A. Singapore English and B. Malaysian English.   It will be noticed that a range of speakers has been introduced, with a wide selection of topics which will give the reader some insight into many aspects of life in Singapore and Malaysia, e.g. language use, occupations, family life, schools, beliefs and attitudes.

The texts in the section on Written English are divided into three sub-sections.   The first sub-section includes impromptu compositions by school children and casual jottings such as notes and messages.   The second sub-section includes advertising leaflets, and menus of restaurants whilst the texts in the third sub-section are mainly advertisements from the press.   English language newpapers in Singapore and Malaysia are, on the whole, written in a type of 'international English'.   Examples of local English can sometimes be found in advertisements and in letters to the editor.

The texts in the section on English in Literature are divided into three sub-sections: A. Poetry, B. Drama and C. Prose.

A great deal of poetry in the region is written in an English which does not in itself give any indication of the writer's origin, although the themes and descriptions may relate to the local situation and to Chinese, Malay and Indian culture.   However, there are a few poems which contain lines reflecting local speech (texts 68-71).

The use of English in drama set in Singapore and Malaysia poses particular problems.   If the characters are such that they would naturally speak a basilectal variety, an audience - especially a non-local audience - may have problems in understanding the dialogue.   The playwright's choice is between full naturalism, at one end of the scale, an 'international' type of English on the other hand or some type of compromise.   There are few local playwrights who have made extensive use of local speech.   One of the few, Edmund Dorall, who shows a fine ability to write dialogue reflecting not only the different types of English used by speakers of different socio-economic background but even variation by the same speaker in different situations, has been criticized for doing so by Lloyd Fernando in his introduction to the volume in which Dorall's play appears. Extracts from Dorall's play 'A Tiger is loose in our Community' are included in this volume (text 72).

There are relatively few prose writers who have used Singapore or Malaysian English in their short stories. Often, the local varieties appear in the form of brief dialogues or monologues by minor characters. Exceptions are the short story by S. Y. Killingley Everything's Arranged (text 74) and some of the short stories of Catherine Lim, particularly The Taximan's Story, which is written entirely in a colloquial SgE (text 75).

In various places in the texts, reference is made to the educational system. In both Singapore and Malaysia, the school system is divided into six years of primary education followed by secondary education. In Singapore, at the end of the 4th year of secondary education (often referred to as Sec Four), students sit for the GCE (General Certificate of Education). Recently, it has been possible for 'slower learners' to complete their GCE in five years. They can sit for the 'Certificate of Secondary Education' after their fourth year and, if they pass, can proceed to the GCE in their fifth year. The highest secondary school examination is the Advanced Levels examination (A levels) which performs the function of a matriculation examination for university entrance.

All the texts in this volume are given in conventional English spelling but some are also given in a broad phonetic notation using the International Phonetics Association (I.P.A.) symbols. In the conventional spelling, consonants which were not realized in speech, unreleased or replaced by a glottal stop have been put in brackets, e.g. subje(cts), an(d), kid(s), tol(d). However, if verbs were given in the stem form instead of the past tense form, this has not been indicated by adding the past tense affix in brackets as it is obvious from the text, e.g. Las(t) year I attend Sec Four an(d) study.....

In dialogues, the letter I refers to the Interviewer.

Each text has been provided with a set of notes as well as general comments on the particular speaker and the text. It is hoped that the texts, besides giving an indication of the range of Singapore and Malaysian English, will reflect something of the life and culture of these two nations.

I. SPOKEN ENGLISH

A. Singapore English

Section (a)

1. Waitress (Hokkien): English and English tuition
2. Salesgirl (Hokkien): School
3. Waitress (Cantonese): Cantonese opera
4. Salesgirl (Cantonese): Sago Lane
5. Taxi driver (Cantonese): Language use in the family
6. Mechanic (Indian-Malay): Motor scooters
7. Kitchenhand (Baba Hokkien): About school
8. Storekeeper and part-time taxi driver (Hokkien): His passengers
9. Odd-job man (Hainanese): About cost of living, children and food
10. Parking warden (Cantonese): Her family and her work
11. Waitress (Hokkien): School
12. Labourer (Malay): His sister and films.

Texts 1-10 are examples of the basilectal end of the Singapore English Speech Continuum (SgE). All the speakers have had English-medium education, ranging from a few years at primary school to four years at secondary school (Secondary Four). None of the Secondary Four speakers has passed the GCE O-Level examination (General Certificate of Examination).

Naturally, the language in the texts varies somewhat according to the sex and age of the speaker and the topic under discussion but all of them display some of the characteristic features of basilectal Singapore English. This means, for instance, a high reduction of consonant clusters and virtually 100% non-occurrence of final stops or replacement by glottal stops, very frequent lack of BE and a high degree of non-marking for noun plural, past tense and third person singular. The aspect marker already for completive aspect is common as is the variable lack of the definite and indefinite articles and object pronouns. These characteristics are also evident, but to a lesser degree, in the later texts, which are examples of mesolectal and acrolectal speech.

In Texts 7-10, where the interviewer uses Colloquial Singapore English, the speakers drop into an even more colloquial style, including the frequent use of particles such as lah, ah and what.

Texts 11 and 12 are of interest as they are borderline cases between basilectal SgE and English spoken as a 'learner's language'. This type of English would be used either by speakers who are English-medium educated but who have a low educational standard and practically no use for English in much of their everyday verbal interaction or by those who have had a non-English-medium education but who have some contact with English-medium educated speakers, usually in the work situation.

It must be emphasized again (see Introduction) that no valid variable analysis for speakers or lects can be carried out on the basis of these excerpts alone. For this, far larger samples are required and the authors' findings on variation in Singapore and Malaysian English (cf. Platt 1977, 1978, 1980, Platt and Weber 1980) are based on a larger corpus of data.

TEXT 1

The following text is from a recorded interview with a twenty year old waitress in a small coffee house in Singapore. She has had an English-medium education up to Secondary Four (the fourth year in secondary school). Her parents are Hokkien. She speaks only Hokkien to her mother and Hokkien and English to her father and her siblings. She uses Hokkien, some Cantonese and English when talking to the other waitresses or to customers.

Singapore parents often make great financial sacrifices to further their children's education. As this case shows, parents of lower socio-economic status could only afford to get a completely untrained private tutor such as the speaker of this text.

a. Comments on English

C: I don'(t) pass my English.   I don'(t) thin(k) so my English is [1] tha(t) goo(d).   Maybe spea(k) now.[2] I can tal(k) well bu(t) written English is no goo(d) - especially the tenses.

I: What did you do in your English classes?

C: Wri(te) composition(s).   Now you have to answer question(s), comprehension, go(t) to do grammar.   They as(k) you grammar.

I: Did you do any English literature?

C: You mean, read story book(s)?   Literature an(d) story books.   This subje(ct), I don'(t) ta(ke).   I study, bu(t) I don'(t) ta(ke) for exam because I know, I am very weak in English.   Especially they ask question(s) I don'(t) know - an(d) my tense(s) go(t) mix(ed) u(p) - so I don'(t) take.   I still remember - one tes(t) I get zero.

b.   Comments on English Tuition

I: And when you finish work here - what do you do?

C: Well, I have job. Tuition to small kid(s). After wor(k) I use to[3]
    go an(d) teach. Teach small children.

I: What do you teach?

C: Eh - English.

I: Ah, how did you get the job?

C: Through frien(ds). I don'(t) advertise. Through frien(ds). They
    recommen(d) to teach.[4] So after teach thém, the mother say - there
    some more kid(s). You li(ke) to teach?[5] I say: yes. So I go
    aroun(d). I go(t) three batch(es)[6] - three batch(es) of children.

I: How old are they?

C: All of thém - very young but one boy is secondary.[7] The res(t) of
    them - all primary.

I: Don't they have English at school?

C: (does not understand) English school?

I: Yes, these children? Do they go to an English school or to a
    Chinese school?

C: One primary kid - from English school, the res(t) from Chinese -
    an(d) one secondáry - English school.[8]

I: How do you teach them? Do you have a text book?

C: No. Suppose, firs(t)ly I as(k) thém wha(t) subje(ct) they li(ke).
    If they say English - ta(ke) ou(t) English boo(ks).[9] As(k) them to
    réad[10] an(d) after that I question thém. Explain firs(t), réad an(d)
    explain. Then I question thém.

I: And if they don't know a word, do you explain it to them in Chinese
    or in English?

C: Tell them in Mandarin. If they don'(t) understan(d), tell them in
    their home diale(ct). If they Cantonese I tell them if I know
    wor(d). If I don'(t) know, then I try, I try to fin(d).

I: Very good. And do they work very hard? Do they do what you tell
    them to?

C: Some of thém, they nice. They behave. They véry obedien(t). Two
    ki(ds), I teach - véry[11] naughty. You go(t) to really scol(d)[12]them.
    So everytime I go(t) fe(d) u(p) - I scol(d) thém. An(d) if they
    don'(t) listen I ta(ke) cane an(d) hit thém.

I: And their parents don't mind?

C: (lively) They don'(t) min(d), they don'(t) min(d). Their paren(ts)
    say: If they naughty, cane them.

Notes

1. Note the use of <u>so</u> as a complementizer.   This is typical in basilectal Singapore and Malaysian English (cf. Platt & Weber 1980).

2. The speaker meant that she is able to use English in conversations.

3. The speaker means here that she <u>teaches</u>.   See comments on aspect markers at the beginning of this section.

4. The speaker meant that her friends recommended her as a teacher.

5. The speaker wanted to imply that the mother of her pupils told her that there were some more children and asked her whether she would like to teach them too.

6. Note the use of <u>batch</u> with animate reference.   In some varieties of English it would be more common with objects rather than people.

7. The speaker meant 'One of the boys attended secondary school'.

8. The speaker meant that one primary child was from an English-medium school and the rest from Chinese-medium schools, except for one child who went to a secondary English-medium school.

9. '...then we take out English books.'

10. 'I ask them to read'

11. The intensifier <u>very</u> is often stressed and the vowel of the first syllable is lengthened [vɛ:ɹi].

12. <u>Scold</u> is used in SgE where many other varieties of English would now use expressions such as <u>tell off</u>, <u>tick off</u>.

TEXT 2

The following text is from a recorded interview with an eighteen year old sales girl in a small shop in Singapore. She has had an English-medium education up to the fourth year in secondary school. Her parents are Hokkien. She speaks mainly Hokkien at home but English to her friends. At work she uses Hokkien, Cantonese and English to the other salesgirls and mainly English to the customers.

The text shows the attitude of a not particularly academically minded girl to her school subjects. As the competition is strong, there is little chance for a girl who fails in some of her subjects in Secondary Four to obtain even a medium-status position.

Interview about school

I: Did you go to an English-medium school or to a Chinese-medium school?

D: I'm from a English school - primary an(d) secondary.

I: How many years did you go to secondary school?

D: Four years.

I: What did you study?

D: I study A-Class.[1] I am from a A-Class.

I: How many subjects did you take?

D: Seven. They - Math, Scien(ce), English.[2] This is compúlsórý - an(d) secon(d) language,[3] of course, we take Chinese,[4] y'see, bu(t) some use to take Malay.[5] Is either u(p) to you whether you ta(ke) wha(t),[6] see.

I: Which subjects did you like best?

D: I li(ke) bes(t) is of course Geography an(d) Chinese.

I: Did you learn Chinese characters?

D: Ya, learn writing - from small we learn writing.

I: How many characters did you learn?

D: Oh tha(t) - a lo(t) - a lo(t), a! - Any we go(t) to use - we have to use, y'see.[7] Bu(t) sometime we forgo(t) wha(t) we go(t) to use an(d) how you going to wri(te) ít.

I: Did you have to write essays in Mandarin?

D: Ya. Essays in Mandarin. Is qui(te) tough - for Mandarin. Leave one stro(ke) only - wrong a(l)ready.[8] One stro(ke) you wro(te) wrong - whole answer wrong.

I: If you leave out one stroke, can it mean another word?

D: Cannó(t)[9] - seldom, véry seldom mean another wor(d).

I: What about Geography? What did you do in Geography?

D: Geography? Geography, I li(ke) learn abou(t) plácés, y'see - either Hong Kong, London. Oh, I li(ke) to learn all aroun(d) the worl(d). Is very interesting, y'see. Is véry nice, Geography.

I: Did you have to do any drawing?

D: Ya, map(s).   We draw map(s).   Distinguish place(s) they cultivate
    rubber or coconu(t) and so on.   Bu(t) 's come to the exam[10] - is véry
    difficul(t).   Is véry difficul(t).

I: What was your final examination called?

D: Ya, final exam is - this depen(ds) - we - up to Lower Sécondárý is
    Cambridge.   Cambridge the las(t) exam for us, see, the Lower Cambridge.

I: Did you sit for all your subjects?

D: This - a(t) leas(t) six subjec(t)s.   Depen(d)s on how many subje(cts)
    we ta(ke), y'see.   But Math, Chinese, English is compúlsórý.   We
    canno(t) - I mean, we canno(t) don'(t) take[11] - all mus(t) take it.
    A(ll) mus(t) ta(ke) - so I too(k) abou(t) six, seven subje(cts).[12]
    I(t) cos(ts) abou(t) fifty dollars over.[13]   One subje(ct) they pay
    for seven dollars.   Two subje(cts) - pay for seven.

I: How long did you have to wait for the results?

D: Oh, the resul(t)s?   Oh - three mon(th)s we have to wai(t) for.   Three,
    four mon(th)s.   Aroun(d) Feb(ru)ary[14] - aroun(d) Feb(ru)ary.

Notes

1. The speaker meant that she was in the A-stream at her school.

2. 'They are Maths, Science and English.'

3. 'as a second language...'

4. Chinese here refers to Mandarin (see introduction).

5. 'but some take Malay.'

6. 'You can take either; it's up to you what you take.'

7. The speaker wanted to say that they had to write in Chinese characters
    in order to make use of the characters they had been taught.

8. 'If you leave out just one stroke, then it is wrong.'

9. The use of 'cannot' instead of expressions such as 'No, it can't' is
    very typical for basilectal SgE.

10. 'When it comes to the exam...'.

11. 'we have to take it...'.

12. 'six or seven subjects.'

13. 'fifty dollars or more.'

TEXT 3

The following text is from a recorded interview with a twenty four year old waitress in a small restaurant in Singapore. She has had an English-medium education up to Secondary Four (the fourth year of secondary school). Her parents are Cantonese. She speaks only Cantonese at home but English with her friends, some of her neighbours and her employer. To customers she uses Cantonese, Hokkien, English or Bazaar Malay.

The text illustrates some aspects of the life of wayang actors in Singapore. Street operas, commonly called wayang in Singapore, were very popular among the Chinese. They were performed on vacant lots or in front of temples on temporary stages. The action is highly formalized and actors wear elaborate costumes and makeup. Each of the main dialect groups has its own repertoire of operas. The popularity of street operas is declining, particularly with the younger age groups.

Cantonese opera in Singapore

W: My paren(t)s job is opera, see.   You know these (this)[1] Chinese opera?

I: Oh, yes.

W: Wayang[2] - ah[3] My parents - opera.[4]   I follow them an(d) watch how they a(ct).   This very big trou(pe), y'see.   Many of us.   Go(t)[5] prince there.   Go(t) the prince - oh - a lo(t)[6], y'see.   Depen(ds) wha(t) wish to a(ct)[7] la.   For my paren(t)s, they use to a(ct)[9] some li(ke) - mother of a princess.   My father - father of a girl an(d) so on.

I: Do your parents own their costumes?

W: Ya, my paren(t)s own.   Bu(t) this depen(d)s.   Some Hokkien, see, Hokkien, they occupy all the costume(s).[10]   Cantonese one is differen(t).[11]   Cantonese one all own(ed) by ourselv(es).   This why[12] pay have to be very high, see.   They give a book to you - wha(t) tomorrow is going on.[13]   Tonigh(t) give you a book.   You have to rea(d) - to memorize all the wor(ds).   After you spea(k) - I spea(k). After I spea(k) - you all spea(k).[14]   You have to memorize all the wor(ds).   Go(t) a man doin(g) in charge,[15] you see.   He give(s) you all the books an(d) tell(s) you.[16]   You read all the nigh(t).   An(d) you have to cry, see.   You have to a(ct), you really crying,[17] y'see. People say: Ah, you a(ct) - you no(t) crying.[18]   Wha(t) is the use, y'know.   People - angry.   Is nothing to see.[19]   An(d) have to sing[20] in very lou(d) voice.   For my mother voice,[21] she very loud. My mother can a(ct) qui(te) goo(d).   I insis(t)[22] she can.   She cry, she cry.   An(d) she preten(d) to be something stupi(d), stupi(d) - funny ty(pe) of girl, y'see.

Notes

1. The use of demonstratives these and this often both realized as either [d̪ðis] or [d̪ði:s], is common in SgE where in other varieties of English either the definite article is used or no article at all, as in the example in the text.

2. The Màlay word <u>wayang</u> refers to various kinds of theatrical performances, as in <u>Wayang Kulit</u> the well-known performances with shadow puppets.   In Singapore in particular, <u>wayang</u> is used for traditional Chinese opera, often performed in the open air.

3. <u>a</u> is a question marker used in Chinese.

4. 'My parents are opera performers.'

5. 'There is a prince.'

6. The speaker means that, in addition to the prince, there are a lot of other characters.

7. 'It all depends on what opera they wish to perform.'

8. The use of <u>la</u> shows here that the speaker is very relaxed and on friendly terms with the interviewer.

9. 'My parents take different parts, such as ...'

10. The speaker meant that, in the case of some Hokkien opera companies, the costumes are owned by the management.

11. 'It is different for Cantonese operas.'

12. '<u>This</u> <u>is</u> why ...'

13. 'They give you a book with the text of the next day's performance.'

14. The speaker meant that everyone has to be familiar with their cues.

15. 'There is a man in charge.'

16. '... and tells you what to do.'

17. 'You have to act as if you are really crying.'

18. 'There you are - acting - but you are not really crying.'

19. 'If the actors are not crying properly, there is nothing worth looking at.'

20. 'And you have to sing ...'

21. 'As for my mother's voice, it is very loud.'

22. It is common for speakers of SgE to intersperse relatively formal words such as <u>insist</u> in informal discourse.

TEXT 4

The following text is from a recorded interview with a twenty year old salesgirl in a small department store in Singapore. She has had an English-medium education up to Secondary Four (the fourth year of secondary school). Her parents are Cantonese from mainland China. At home, she speaks Cantonese to her parents and Cantonese and English with her siblings. She speaks mainly Hokkien with the girls at work and Hokkien, Cantonese, English or Bazaar Malay to the customers according to their education and ethnic background.

The text illustrates some of the atmosphere of Sago Lane. Sago Lane was once a well-known street in Chinatown with roadside stalls and the typical old two- or three-storey shophouses, with little shops open to the street. Now re-development has taken place in the area and many of the shophouses of Sago Lane have been demolished to make room for high-rise buildings.

Sago Lane

Sago La(ne) - véry góo(d). I mean, for foreigns[1] they li(ke) to go
segɔ le   vɛːɹi gu   aɩ min fɔ fɔɹəns d̥ə̃e laɩ? tu go

there an(d) see or márkétíńg[2] an(d) so on. A(ll) those ol(d) lady there
d̥ɛə ən si ɔ maketiŋ ən so ɔn ɔ   d̥os ɔl ledi d̥ɛə

they shouting an(d) as(k) you to buy their thing(s). They shouting.
de ʃaᵒtiŋ æn as ju tu baⁱ d̥ə̃ɛə t̬θiŋ   d̥ə̃ɛˡ ʃaᵒtiŋ

Sometime[3] you don'(t) buy their thing(s), sco(ld) a(t) you, see. They
samtaˡ ju d̥ɔᵒ baˡ d̥ə̃ɛˡ t̬θiŋ skɔ æ? ju si d̥ə̃e

can sco(ld) a(t) you, really sco(ld). Even Singaporeans they sco(ld),[4]
kɛn skɔ æ? ju ɹɛli skɔ   ivən siŋapɔɹiⁱəns d̥ə̃e skɔ

you know; no(t) only foreign(s). You - a foreigns,[5] you can[6] buy things,
ju nɔ   nɔ? onli fɔɹən   ju ə fɔɹenz ju kən baˡ t̬iŋz

they charge you expensive. Don'(t) know,[7] they charge yóu fór double
d̥e tʃadʒ ju ekspensif d̥ou nɔ d̥ə̃e tʃadʒ ju fɔ dabəl

price. Singaporean(s), we know. We sco(ld) ba(ck) a(t) thém. Know
pɹaˡs siŋapɔɹiⁱəⁿ wi nɔ wi skɔ bæ? æ? d̥ə̃em nɔ

wha(t) to pay, a. Is qui(te) chea(p) la. Chinatown qui(te) chea(p),
wɔ? tu pe a is kwaˡ? tʃi? la tʃaˡnətaᵒn kwaˡ? tʃi?

(you) know.
    nɔ

Notes

1. 'foreigners'

2. 'and do marketing ...'

3. 'If you don't buy ...'

4. 'They even scold Singaporeans.'

5. 'If you are a foreigner ...'   Note the conditional construction without the use of if.

6. can is used here to express something like 'and if you happen to buy there.'

7. 'As (or) because you don't know, they charge you double the price.'

TEXT 5

The following text is from a recorded interview with a forty year old taxidriver.   He has had an English-medium education up to Primary Three (the third year of primary school) but has picked up English when talking to English speaking passengers.

The text gives some good insights into language use in Singapore. Although the speaker is Cantonese, the main dialect spoken at home is Hokkien because the speaker's wife and mother-in-law are Hokkien and so are his neighbours.   However, he does speak some Cantonese with his children.   It also illustrates one of the ways in which basilectal Singapore English is transmitted by parents and older siblings to children even before they enter school.

Language use in the family

I: What did you talk before you went to school?

T: Firs(t) language - Cantonese.   I study English abou(t) three years only.   I all learn in driving taxi[1] an(d) all tha(t).

I: How many years did you go to school?

T: Abou(t) three, four years only.   I thin(k) is primary three, I thin(k).

I: Did you learn any Chinese at school?

T: Chinese? One, two years I thin(k).   Bu(t) spea(k) some Chinese.[2] Spea(k) Cantonese, Hokkien, English, Malay also.   In Singapore, we - a lo(t) of language(s).[3]

I: What do you speak at home?

T: A(t) home, we spea(k) Hokkien because my wife - Hokkien, see. She's Chinese educáted.[4]

I: Does she know any English?

T: English? She don'(t) know. She only know Chinese only. Bu(t) my son - English school.[5] I spea(k) with my son sometime I spea(k) English.[6] I li(ke) him to learn more fastes(t) spea(k) English.

I: You have only one son?

T: Ah, have two son(s). One no(t) ye(t) going to school. Maybe en(d) of this year - going to kindergarten.

I: Does he know any English?

T: Don'(t) know.[7] But now I starting train him. Mus(t) teach him how to spea(k) English. Tha(t)s why the going to school is more easy.[8] Spea(k) Hokkien a(t) home.[9] Wife's mother, mother-in-law, y'know, she's staying[10] with me. She speak(s) Hokkien 'cause she's a Hokkien peoples. Canno(t) spea(k) any Mandarin, because she's old lady.[11]

I: But you yourself are Cantonese?

T: Ya, for myself is Cantonese.

I: Do you sometimes talk to your sons in Cantonese?

T: Yes, yes, tal(k) wi(th) my son(s) in Cantonese.

I: Do you know any Teochew?

T: Teochew, don'(t) know. 'Cause we are something like we're neighbours, we don'(t) have Teochews.[12] Only have Hokkiens. Tha(t) why we don'(t) know how to spea(k). Understand but don'(t) spea(k).[13]

Notes

1. 'I picked up all my English during my time as taxidriver.'

2. The speaker is referring to <u>Mandarin</u>.

3. 'we <u>have</u> a lot of languages.'

4. The speaker's wife went to a Chinese-medium school, where the language of instruction was Mandarin. See Introduction.

5. 'But my son goes to an English-medium school.'

6. 'When I speak with my son, I sometimes speak English.'

7. The speaker means that his younger son doesn't know English.

8. The speaker means that he is teaching his younger son some English so that it will be easier for the boy at school.

9. 'We speak Hokkien at home.'

10. <u>Stay</u> is used in Singapore English for <u>live</u>.

11. The speaker means that when his mother-in-law was young there was little opportunity for many Chinese, particularly girls, to attend school at all and so she did not learn Mandarin.

12. 'There are no Teochews among our neighbours.'

13. 'We understand Teochew but we don't speak it.'

TEXT 6

The following text is from a recorded interview with a thirty-eight year old mechanic.   He has had an English-medium education up to Secondary Two (the second year of secondary school).   His father is Indian and his mother Malay.   Both the speaker and his wife are of a Jawi Peranakan background, i.e. they are descendants of Indians who came to Malaya or the Straits Settlements, married Malay women and adopted to some extent the Malay culture and language without completely losing their Indian identity.   The speaker claimed knowledge of "a little Indian" but at home uses Malay to his wife and children and some English to his eldest child who attends an English-medium school.

About motor   scooters

I: How do you come to work?

N: I come on scóotér.

I: Isn't it a bit dangerous in this weather?   (It was raining heavily on that day).

N: Ah, we mus(t) wear safety helme(t), y'know.

I: Can you take a pillion passenger?

N: Can.   'Cause I qualifie(d)[1] my driving líceñce.   You have to ta(ke) highway co(de) tes(t).   Then you have to ta(ke) driving tes(t).   Then you can go to.[2]

I: Isn't it compulsory for the pillion passenger to wear a helmet?

N: Helmet?   Ya, helmet must.[3]

I: Do you have L-plates here?

N: Ya, L mean, we jus(t) learning.

Notes

1.   'I qualified for my driving licence.'

2.   'Then you can (are allowed to) drive a scooter.'

3.   'Yes, a helmet must be worn.'

TEXT 7

The following text is from a recorded interview with a thirty-six year old kitchen hand. She went to an English-medium primary girls' school where she sat for her PSLE (Primary School Leaving Examination) but did not pass it. Her parents are both Babas (Straits-born Chinese). She uses Hokkien and Baba Malay with her parents, children and husband. She uses Hokkien and some English with her friends and at her place of work.

The text illustrates that the speaker is an expressive speaker of basilectal Singapore English. She relives the experiences of her school-days and her fears of incurring her mother's displeasure is vividly captured in this excerpt.

About the type of discipline at school

I: If some girls are naughty, all of you have to stay back?

R: Yah, for the sa(k)e of them, they have to stay ba(ck).[1]   I have to including too lah![2]   The whole class have to stay ba(ck) lah!

I: What sort of explanation did you give to your mother?

R: Tha(t)'s why I to(ld) my mother[3] - say - aah.

I: She believed you?

R: Yah she believe me.   I say - "For the sa(k)e of my gir(l)s[4] - one ma(k)e mista(k)es,[5] we have to stay you see - you -" "May be you is the one doing".[6]   I say, "No I'm not".   An(d) then[7] I wen(t) to schoo(l).   In the morning I to(ld) my teacher.   I say, "If an - any girl ma(ke) you troubel, you please gi(ve) me go home lah,[8] because ah - I never ma(ke) any troubels 'know.[9]   The the teacher to(ld) me say,[10] "I canno(t) gi(ve) you alone go home.[11]   If I gi(ve) you alone go home - wha(t) the girls wi(ll), the studen(ts) wi(ll) say to me.[12]   Tha(t) means I'm a teacher very unfair".[13]   Aah, then I explain(ed) to my gir(l)s all lah, my colleague(s) all.[14]   I say, "You please lah, mus(t) listen to teacher.   Wha(t) teacher as(ks) you to do, you do it lah.   If you canno(t) you ta(lk) to them[15] nicely. May be he[16] wi(ll) say, 'OK, may be - tsk - OK nex(t) time you try your bes(t) or wha(t) lah'".[17]   Then slowly slowly, they wi(ll) - tsk - li(ke) - tz - say listen what I say.[18]   I say - I to(ld) her,[19] I say, "You wan(t) to ma(ke)s frien(d) with me, I ma(ke) very frien(d) frien(d)ly to you lah".[20]   An(d) then because why, - for the sa(ke), one of the gir(l)s ma(ke) mista(ke), I have to stay.   I say, "My mother every time sco(ld) me say[21] "I'm running ou(t)si(d)e playing foo(l)[22] or wha(t).

I: Er er.

R: An(d) my - my mother is o(ld) fashion type of peopéls 'know; olden days peopél.[23]

I: Er huh.

R: Aah - young gir(l)s canno(t) go ou(t) la(te)ly;[24] come ba(ck) schoo(l), mus(t) immedia(t)ely[25] - li(k)e say one thirty - tha(t) means reach schoo(l) mus(t) be - aah - reach home mus(t) be two or one forty fi(v)e li(ke) that.   If you go home by bus - la(te) - la(te) litter bi(t) lah[26] - you have to wai(t) - because bus every time queue up.

I: Hmmm.

R: All my frien(d) all say, "OK I try - I try to chan(g)e lah.   Li(ke)
    say - tsk - "Try to control mysel(f) not to be ru(de) to the teachers[27]
    all rah".   I say "I ho(p)e so - tha(t)'s all".

Notes

1.   'Because of these girls, we all had to stay back.'

2.   'myself included'

3.   'for this reason I told my mother'

4.   'Because of the girls in my class'

5.   The speaker means one of them misbehaved or was unsatisfactory in
     her work.

6.   The mother said that she could have been the culprit.

7.   'the next day'

8.   'would you please let me go home'

9.   'you know'

10. 'and said'

11. 'I can't allow only you to go home'

12. 'what will the students say to me'

13. 'That would mean, I'm a very unfair teacher'

14. 'to all my classmates'

15. 'the teacher(s)'

16. Most likely she. Note that the speaker does not always make the
     distinction between masculine or feminine third person singular.

17. The speaker means that the teacher would say "just try to do your
     best", or something like that.

18. 'Then gradually they did listen to what I said.'

19. 'the main trouble maker'

20. 'If you want to be friends with me I can be a good friend to you.'

21. 'My mother scolds me and says ...'

22. The speaker means that her mother thought she was not in school but
     having fun elsewhere.

23. The speaker means that her mother is an old-fashioned type of person.

24. It was the mother's view that young girls should not stay out.

25. 'must come back straight from school'

26. 'you would be a bit later if you took a bus'

27. The speaker means that after her "pep-talk" her classmates responded
     and said that they would try to be better behaved in future.

TEXT 8

The following text is from a recorded interview with a thirty-one year old storekeeper and part-time taxi-driver. He did not pass his PSLE (Primary School Leaving Examination) and left school after that. He is Hokkien and speaks Hokkien with his parents and Hokkien and Mandarin with his wife and children. He watches mainly Chinese TV programmes and goes to Chinese movies because his wife was educated at a Chinese-medium school. He uses Hokkien and Cantonese at his place of work as a store-keeper and speaks English only with some of his passengers.

The text illustrates aspects of being a taxi driver in Singapore. The most common taxis in Singapore are those of the NTUC (National Trades Union Congress). They are light blue in colour. All taxis in Singapore have a meter and the use of meters is compulsory. The receiving of a commission for taking tourists to certain shops is, of course, illegal.

a.   Commenting on his passengers and other taxi drivers

C: Passenger(s) depen(d) lah - good one(s) also go(t), bad one(s) also go(t).[1]   Some ah[2] some taxi driver(s) they wan(t) to go to this touris(t) area(s) like hotel(s) ah. They par(k) there, y'know. Then if the touris(ts) want to go and buy things, buy anything ah, they book the taxi say one hour I pay you how much.[3] Then after that they brough(t) the passenger(s) go and buy thing(s) already.[4]   Then the shop(s) ah give commission to the taxi driver(s) lah. Don'(t) know how many per cen(t).

I: You don'(t) wan(t) to do this type of business ah?

C: No lah! Don'(t) wan(t) to do this type. Wha(t) for? No use one.[5] You was(te) the time there - si(t) down and wai(t) wai(t) wai(t), sometime also no touris(t) came ou(t) wha(t).[6]

I: Do you charge more during Chinese New Year?

C: No lah! Where can charge more![7] Canno(t) charge more! Depen(d) lah if the passenger goo(d) jus(t) like the meter fare is two fifty OK, they give you three dollar(s). No nee(d) to ta(k)e the chan(ge).[8]

b.   Relating how he was involved in an accident

I: Your wife told me you had an accident yesterday.

C: Yesterday ah - aah - seven something ah. I wan(t) to go ba(ck) to ta(ke) my dinner lah. I ta(ke) one - one - passenger to this - ah Eas(t) Coas(t) Loa(d)[9] lah and then he drop down[10] lah and then I do(n't) wan(t) - I wan(t) to take a rest lah. Then I - ah - return home here. Then up to Katong Shopping[11] there ah, the traffi(c) ligh(ts) go re(d) y'know and then I sto(p) and then a(t) the ba(ck) - the - go(t) two car(s) bang me. One car bang me and then the thir(d) one bang the secon(d) one. An(d) jus(t) now I go and repor(t) the insurance.

Notes

1. 'there are good ones and bad ones.'

2. <u>ah</u> is used here as an emphatic marker.

3. 'I'll pay you so much per hour.'

4. 'the passengers are taken to the shops and straightaway they're buying things.'

5. 'It's no use.'

6. <u>what</u> - emphatic marker often expressing some annoyance or dis-approval.

7. 'How can I charge more!'

8. if the passenger is generous; he gives three dollars for a two dollar fifty meter fare and doesn't want any change back.

9. 'East Coast Road'

10. 'he gets out'

11. Katong Shopping Centre. Katong is a suburb in the southeastern part of Singapore.

TEXT 9

The following text is from a recorded interview with a forty year old odd-job man in an office. He has had five years of primary education in an English-medium school. He is Hainanese and speaks Hainanese to his parents, siblings and relatives. His wife is a Cantonese. He uses Mandarin and Cantonese with her and his children and English, Cantonese and Hainanese at his place of work.

The text illustrates the speaker's views on the cost of living in Singapore and the problems of bringing up children. In the third part of the text the speaker talks about 'chicken rice' served at a particular restaurant. 'Chicken rice' is a particular Hainanese dish, consisting of rice cooked in chicken broth, chicken pieces and a sauce made up of chillies, garlic, ginger and lime.

a.   About poorly paid jobs

R: Bu(t) now in XXX(name of his firm) you know - they ge(t) jo(b) easy
wha(t).[1]   Bu(t) those wages sta(ff)[2] - can ge(t) easy lah![3]   Only
two or three four hundred dollars,[4] where go(t) enou(gh) nowadays[5] -
standar(d) of living[6] so high righ(t) or no(t)?   Where go(t) enou(gh)
righ(t) or no(t)?[7]   You see jus(t) imagine - bus fare, transpor(t)
money, your lunch, your dinner - finish already wha(t).[8]   Wha(t)
happen you wan(t) to marry[9] - how - canno(t) - wi(fe) - canno(t) marry
wha(t).[10]   Really you know - damn difficul(t) you know - wan(t) house

ren(t) ah[11] - li(k)e tha(t)[12] water bi(ll) come ah - a(ll) this
compulsory thing you have to pay righ(t) or no(t) - water bi(ll), house
ren(t), a(ll) this thing, makan,[13] foo(d) lodging ah - 300 dollars
where go(t) enou(gh) - tell me?

b.   Bringing up children

I: You teach the children or is it the mother?

R: Mother lah!   Mother to teach lah.   Where - where - where go(t) time
to teach[14] - come to wor(k) already, what time go ba(ck) home.
Already wha(t) time already lah - already - already, already wha(t)
time already already.   By the time la(te) see already wha(t)[15]

I: Your wife doesn't work lah?

R: No, never wor(k)

I: Your children take tuition or not?

R: They ta(ke) wha(t)![16]   Ever! - wha(t) they wan(t) I jus(t) gi(ve) them
wha(t) .... anything lah!   Wha(t)ever they wan(t) jus(t) gi(ve)
them - small chil(d)ren mus(t) gi(ve) them freedom wha(t).[17]   But one
thing, too much freedom, you will spoil him.[18]

I: But the mother is strict?

R: Depen(ds) on wha(t) kin(d) of thing lah.   Wha(t) they ta(ke) mos(t)ly -
a(ll) sor(t) of thing lah - they - .   Now you know - mus(t) - a(ll)
the chil(d)ren you contro(l) them ah - they wi(ll) ma(ke) enemy of
you,[19] righ(t) or no(t)?

I: Oh dear!

R: Yah wha(t)!   If don'(t) - wan(t) to go where - you don'(t) o(b)je(ct)
him ah.   I thin(k) waah you - righ(t) or no(t)?[20]

c.   About chicken rice served at XXX restaurant

I: You know XXX Chicken Rice?   Not famous anymore is it?

R: I don'(t) know.   Bu(t) qui(te) a lo(t) of business - no(t) ba(d)
li(ke) tha(t) wha(t).   Actually only the name lah!   Always li(ke)
.... a(ll) chicken is the same wha(t) - righ(t) or no(t)?   Er
XXX - Li(ke) you go to - everybody Tenkuchy Chicken[21] or anything or
XXX Rice - all the name man![22] Plus expensi(ve).   Only for touris(ts)
wha(t).   The name lah - whose the - mos(t)ly mos(t)ly the thing only
the name wha(t).   For instan(ce) you wear the jean(s) ah - a(ll)
jean(s) is the same - only you pu(t) the bran(d) there only righ(t) - .
You see, a(ll) the same wha(t) - tha(t)'s why ...... only the bran(d)
name ma(ke) money only wha(t).   Is true or no(t) - you go an(d)
fin(d) out.   Sometime the bran(d) is - Waah! this very goo(d) -
everybody buy ah.   So the fellow ma(ke) good money wha(t).   Actually
a(ll) thing is the same.   Chicken you see - li(ke) wha(t) wha(t)'s
so special abou(t) XXX Chicken?   Our chicken also the same - a(ll)
came from one chicken righ(t) or no(t)?   Wha(t)'s so specia(l)?
Their name famous, so they ma(ke) money lah!   A(l)ways li(ke) tha(t)
wha(t)!

Notes

1. A marker suggesting 'you ought to know'.

2. He is referring to low paid jobs.

3. 'are easy to get'.

4. 'two, three or four hundred dollars'

5. 'that certainly isn't enough these days'

6. 'cost of living'

7. 'Don't you agree, that's certainly not enough'.

8. The speaker means that once you have paid for all these things, you've used up all your income.

9. 'What happens if you want to marry?'

10. The speaker means on that salary one couldn't support a wife.

11. 'you need to pay the house rent'

12. 'that sort of thing'

13. Malay word for eat. Probably the speaker means 'eating prepared meals away from home', e.g. lunch at food stalls.

14. 'How would I have the time to teach!'

15. The speaker is emphasizing that he really has no time to teach his children because he goes to work early in the morning and returns home late; therefore the repetition of already.

16. 'They certainly do!'

17. 'You must give small children some freedom, of course.'

18. 'But if you give too much freedom, you will spoil him (them).'

19. The speaker means that if you are too strict with your children they will rebel.

20. The speaker means if a child wants to go somewhere and his parents prevent him from going - you can't imagine what the consequences would be!

21. 'Kentucky Chicken'

22. 'You pay for the name.'

TEXT 10

The following text is from a recorded interview with a twenty-nine year old parking warden. Both her parents are Straits-born Chinese (Babas) and she uses Hokkien and Baba Malay with her parents. She speaks Mandarin and Hokkien with her children and husband who is a Hakka. She uses English, Hokkien, Malay and Mandarin with her friends, colleagues and with motorists.

The text illustrates the system of public car parking in Singapore. A motorist who parks his car in a public parking lot is required to display parking coupons in one of the windows of his car. If he forgets to put up a coupon or if he exceeds the time limit shown on the coupon, he will be fined or given a summons. At the time of the interview the two authorities which issue coupons are the HDB (Housing Development Board) for parking places on highrise housing estates and the URA (Urban Redevelopment Authority) for city and suburban parking areas.

a. About her family

I: One boy, one girl. Oh, you're very lucky! Going to have some more?

H: No! I willing to stop lah! Family planning lah! No poin(t) to have more kids lah - because we thin(k) of working ah[1] so we have not time with the kids lah. Because sometime ah - if school holiday(s) I sure go ba(ck) to them y'know. But la(ck) of lo(ve), I know - la(ck) of love you know because mother working ah.

I: Who looks after them?

H: My mother. I got very kin(d) mother. Loo(k) after the kids.

I: You only have the night with them?

H: No nigh(t) no. I daytime wen(t) ba(ck)[2] y'know - they living with my mother.

I: So how often do you see them?

H: Oh - after wor(k) - one wee(k) three four time(s) so I wen(t) there after wor(k) I go there straigh(t) away. Aroun(d) eigh(t) - er - er - wai(t) my husban(d) over there after work[3] or we go later about fi(ve). Aroun(d) eigh(t) o'clo(ck) nine o'clo(ck) then he fetch me ba(ck).[4]

I: Can you tell me something about your little girl? Is she always a good girl?

H: She's a goo(d) gir(l). She li(ke) wha(t), you know.[5] She li(ke) the mo(st) is drawing 'know. The Denni(s) Denni(s) storie(s).

I: So you buy lots of comics for her?

H: No, I di(d)n(t) buy comic(s). She li(ke) to watch every cartoon programme. So the cartoon, daylight, she draw the Dennis face. (laughter) The gir(l), she li(ke) to draw y'know. Whenever she see pretty gir(l), she li(ke) to draw ou(t).[6] I'm very happy tha(t) she can o(b)ser(ve) thing(s) and draw i(t) qui(t)e near the - the girl[7] - and she very goo(d) also lah.[8] I thin(k) firs(t) year - er - in Kindergarten she go(t) firs(t) in standar(d) - hundred percen(t) and

hundred percen(t).   I qui(t)e sati(s)fie(d) abou(t) her.   This fatty
gir(l)s y'know.   She's fa(t), plum(p), big roun(d) eyes like Dennis.
I thin(k) I have a photo of hers - I can let you see.   Nice, round,
y'know, as before and now she's quite tall a bi(t) OK, but she's very
obedien(t) gir(l)s, y'know - you tell her what.[9]   You tell her you
mus(t) give her a reason why.   Because she was brough(t) up - always
I give her reason(s).   Habi(t) lah!

I: You watch Kungfu TV programmes, fighting ones, Mandarin ones ...?[10]

H: Mandarin one(s) I don'(t) have very much time because ah, sometime I
      spend my time croosei[11] lah! Peopél sometime ah, they as(k) me to
      croosei.   Par(t)-time work lah - croosei 'know.

I.   Oh...

H: - er - croosei for T-shir(ts) ladies T-shir(ts) - aah - I go(t) no
      very much time.[12]

I: You charge a lot?

H: No. Jus(t) to - as a frien(d).   Jus(t) to ta(k)e a few dollars for
      the eyesigh(t) wor(k) (laughter).   I learn 'know croosei - making
      dress(es) li(k)e tha(t) lah.

I: You can make clothes ah?

H: Can, I can

I: You got learn or not?[13]

H: Las(t) time[14] pro(bab)ly we were school time.   Because I not very
      goo(d) in studie(s) lah!   So learning for this - for my - for my -
      spare time[15] lah - clothes, like dresses, - aah - man pan(ts), dresses.

b.   Talking about her work

H: We are no more Parking Attenden(ts) collecting fees, now we go roun(d)
      supervise.   We go out and summon cars 'know, and o(b)ser(ve) those
      who never pu(t) coopoon(s).[16]   Now they train us lah - to go out and
      summon - who don'(t) pu(t) coopoon(s).

I: What's the difference between HDB[17] and URA[18] coupons?

H: The differences is there y'know.   The URA they go(t) two section(s),
      the outer zone and the res(tr)icted zone.   Res(tr)icted zo(ne) where
      we all have to come in, we pay four dollars if don'(t) have four
      person(s) per hea(d) in the car, is it?[19]   Aah - there lah - er -
      call a - mean - a res(tr)icted zone lah.[20]   So the charges will be
      higher y'know.   One hour eighty cen(ts), half an hour forty cen(ts).
      So the outsi(de) zone is forty cen(ts) hourly ah. - Where the car
      par(k), they draw in white 'know - the outsi(d)e zone.[21]   An(d) in
      the res(tri)cted zone, they draw in yellow, all the par(ks) they draw
      in yellow.   They go(t) only two section(s).   Some is whole day car-
      park(s) which you pay two forty.

Notes

1. <u>ah</u> is used here as an emphatic marker

2. 'I go back during the daytime.' The speaker means "I go during the day to my mother's place and visit them".

3. 'I wait for my husband there after work'

4. 'Then he picks me up and takes me home'.

5. 'You know what she likes?'

6. 'Whenever she sees a pretty girl she likes to draw her.'

7. 'Her drawing is a good replica of the girl.'

8. 'and she is good in her schoolwork too.'

9. 'if you tell her what to do.'

10. 'programmes in Mandarin?'

11. 'crocheting'

12. 'I don't have much time.'

13. 'Were you taught?'

14. 'At that time...'

15. 'in my spare time'

16. The speaker means that the parking wardens fine the drivers of cars who do not display parking coupons in their windows.

17. Housing Development Board.

18. Urban Redevelopment Authority.

19. All cars entering the Restricted Zone (Inner City) must have at least four occupants. Otherwise a special fee must be paid.

20. 'That area is called a restricted zone.'

21. 'In the outside zone, the parking spaces are marked by white lines.'

TEXT 11

The following text is from a recorded interview with a nineteen year old waitress at a small coffee house. She has had a Chinese-medium education up to Secondary Four (fourth year of secondary school). She has taken English as a compulsory second language. Her parents are Hokkien. She speaks only Hokkien to her parents and elder brothers and sisters. She sometimes speaks English to her younger siblings, who go to an English-medium school. She passed in only four subjects at GCE (General Certificate of Education).

About her school

I: Was your school a big school?

Y: Ya, near my home. Have Chinese péopél Malay péopél also.[1]

I: The first language was Chinese?

Y: Ya, Chinese, ya. Second langridge Engrish.[2] I am Chinese educátéd, canno(t) spea(k) Engrish very well. Sorry, if I canno(t) spea(k).[3] Sorry.

I: Oh, but you <u>can</u> speak it. Your English is much better than my Chinese.

Y; (laugh) I try to spea(k).

I: Did you only have Chinese teachers in your school?

Y: No, have Engrish an(d) Chinese teáchér(s).

I: English teachers too?

Y: Ya, an(d) Malay teacher also. Malay teacher teach Malay, English teacher teach English.

I: Where did the English teachers come from? From England or Australia?

Y: No - lócál péopél. English teacher(s) are Chinese, come from Nanyang,[4] I thin(k).

I: What did you do in English?

Y: Read grámmár. How to spea(k) ah.[5] How to spea(k) Engrish.

I: Did you read stories in English?

Y: Ya, sometime rea(d) some story bóo(ks) - how to do some comprehension, comprehension. Composition lah.[6]

I: What did you write in your compositions?

Y: Ah, easy lah. You know, abou(t) myselfs or anything.

I: Do you know any Malay?

Y: No I don'(t). Ah, a lítél bi(t). I know how to hear.[7] If peopel - ah - say wha(t) - búllý mé or ta(lk) nónseńse, I know how to hear. (laugh). Can use Malay in shop(s), buy some fish, buy fish or buy anything.

I: What did you learn in history?

Y: Abou(t) China. Abou(t) Australia. They all have to wor(k). They

all have to do anything lah.   They - animal(s)[8] - a lot of animal(s).
A lot of how to do.   How to tran(s)por(t).[9]

Notes

1. 'There were Chinese (pupils) and also Malay.'

2. 'the second language was English.'

3. Sorry, if I can't speak it.

4. Nanyang University was the Chinese-medium University of Singapore.
    Now it has been integrated with the University of Singapore to form
    the National University of Singapore where the medium of instruction
    is English.

5. ah is used as an emphatic marker. See Introduction.

6. 'We did some exercises in comprehension and did compositions.'

7. 'I can understand a little.'

8. 'They have animals.'

9. The speaker means that they learned something about industry and
    transport in Australia.

TEXT 12

The following text is from a recorded interview with a twenty-five year old labourer.   He has had a Malay-medium education up to Secondary Two (second year at secondary school).   He took English as a compulsory second language.   His parents are Malay and he speaks Malay to them and to his siblings.   At work, he uses English and Malay and he also speaks English with his Indian and Chinese friends.

The text shows that Singapore English is not only the English used by Singapore Chinese.   The speaker, a Malay, uses some expressions and syntactic constructions which are typical for basilectal Singapore English, such as the completive aspect marker <u>already</u>, the locative ex- istential <u>got</u>, <u>last time</u> (meaning 'formerly').

a.   About his sister

I: Is it a good job to be a nurse in Singapore?

K: No(t) bad - is very good also.

I: Long hours?

K: (did not understand the question) Ya, abou(t) eigh(t) years she work already.[1]

I: Does she have to work very late at night?

K: She's go(t) the shif(t), y'see.[2]   From morning seven o'clo(ck) to two.   So[3] from two to nine o'clo(ck).   After[4] nine to seven o'clock in the morning.

I: Are her patients very difficult to look after?

K: Ya, very.   A lo(t) of people sometime like this thing - sometime don'(t) like.

I: Do nurses wear uniforms here?

K: Ya, white an(d) they all usually - green bel(t).[5]   They all go(t) green bel(t), yellow belt an(d) red one.[6]   Mean li(ke) our company see labourer, clerk - all li(ke) tha(t) lah.[7]

I: Which is the lowest?

K: The green bel(t).   Is called the staff nurse.

I: What comes next?

K: Staff nurse, matron, a lo(t), lah.

I: Your sister is a staff nurse?

K: Is a staff nurse.   Is studying.

b.   About films

I: What do you do after work?

K: After work sometime I go pictures, see my friend(s) an(d) maybe play- ing foo(t)ball or anything.

I: What sort of pictures do you like?

K: I li(ke) the - maybe Hollywood filmstar.

I: You like comedy or drama?

K: I li(ke) the - maybe comba(t) story an(d) detective ah - Western.

I: Are there any Malay pictures?

K: Ya, also go(t) Malay.[8]   Now in Singapore lo(t) of Indonesian filem.
    From Indonesian.

I: Films don't come from Malaysia?

K: Sometime - don'(t) know Malaysia.[9]   Las(t) time[10] a lo(t).

Notes

1. 'Yes, she's been working for about 8 years.'   Note the use of <u>already</u>
    as a <u>completive aspect</u> marker.   See Introduction.

2. 'She works shifts.'

3. <u>So</u> is used where in some varieties of English <u>then</u> would be used.

4. <u>after</u> signifies the third shift, that is "and finally there is the
    nine to seven o'clock shift".

5. 'and most of them have a green belt.'

6. Signifies rank hierarchy as indicated by different colours in belts.

7. The speaker is comparing the hierarchy among the nurses with that in
    the company where he works.

8. 'There are also Malay films.' Note the use of the locative existential
    <u>got</u>.

9. 'I don't think there are so many from Malaysia.'

10. <u>last time</u> = formerly. This is a typical expression in Singapore
    English.

I. SPOKEN ENGLISH

A. Singapore English
Section (b)

13. Store supervisor (Hokkien): Chinese dialects and occupations

14. Salesman (Hainanese): His father

15. Secretary (Hakka): Language

16. Sales representative (Tamil): Cleanliness and smoking

17. Female clerk (Cantonese): Chinese writing

18. Sales manager (Hokkien): Danger in a foreign city

19. Nurse (Teochew): A patient

20. Business executive (Teochew): Chinese in English-medium schools

---

Texts 13-20 are examples of mesolectal to acrolectal speech, with the speaker in text 13 being near the lower end of the mesolect and the speaker in text 20 an example of acrolectal Singapore English. As can be seen, many of the speakers still have the typical features of SgE which have been mentioned with regard to the basilectal speakers, but to a lesser degree. For example, there is a greater occurrence of BE, third person singular, past tense and noun plural marking and a wider range of vocabulary is used. The use of very formal vocabulary is also noticeable.

Text 20 shows that, although acrolectal speakers of SgE come close to Standard British English with regard to syntactic structures, some of their phonetic features are still distincly Singaporean, e.g. replacement of final stop by glottal stop, vowel quality, stress patterns.

TEXT 13

The following text is from a recorded interview with a thirty-two
year old store supervisor. He has had an English-medium education up to
Secondary Four. His parents are Hokkien. They were both English-medium
educated. He speaks English to his father and English and Hokkien to his
mother. He also speaks English to his wife and most of his friends.
This explains why, although he failed in some of his subjects at GCE
(General Certificate of Education), his English has often more mesolectal
qualities than that of speakers in other texts who had the same level of
education (Secondary Four) but less opportunity to speak English.

The text illustrates how in former times different ethnic groups or
subgroups, e.g. Muslim Indians, Hindu Indians, Cantonese, Hokkien and
Teochew Chinese lived in different parts of Singapore and often specialized
in different occupations, e.g. Cantonese goldsmiths, Hainanese cooks,
Shanghainese tailors, Indian textile merchants.

Chinese dialects and occupations

I speak Hokkien but very seldom, you see. Because my family, everybody
is educated in English. I only speak Hokkien only to my servan(t). So
to my friends an(d) anybody else, the majority, I speak only English.
Unless to hawkers or what,[1] depending on their dialects individually, then
I speak to thém accordingly. Majority shopkeepers[2] are Teochew an(d)
Hokkien. Cantonese are mos(t)ly - they deal in - some in this goldsmith shops,[3] you know. An(d) Hakka - also goldsmith. So according -
a lot of Singaporeans are Chinese - and according to their dialects some
of thém, mostly you can judge them in - what do you call it - their oc-
cupation. Teochew people - in offices. For the younger generation is
different. There's a lot of mixture in fact because mos(t) of the young-
sters depending on qualifications. We apply the job,[4] you know, an(d)
then, if we get, then wor(k) fírs(t).[5] Whatever comes first then we have
to go ahead, you see, instead of wasting time. Not all the business
péopél are Hokkien. In fact, there are also péopél from India, merchants of
- some of them are very rich also. That is High Street[6] - so all depends, you see, got many races.[7]

Notes

1. 'to hawkers and people like that.' In Singapore, the term <u>hawkers</u> is
   used for people running stalls where food or drinks are sold.

2. 'The majority of shopkeepers.'

3. The speaker means that most of the goldsmiths are Cantonese.

4. 'We apply for a job ...'

5. 'if we get it, we work first at that one.'

6. High Street is in the older part of Singapore. There are many Indian
   shops there.

7. He means that there are many races in Singapore.

TEXT 14

The text is from a recorded interview with a twenty-nine year old salesman in a small shop. He has had a Chinese-medium primary education and an English-medium secondary education up to Secondary Four. His parents are Hainanese and he speaks Hainanese to them. He speaks mainly Chinese dialects (Hokkien, Cantonese, Hainanese and Hakka) to his customers but he often speaks English to some of the other salesmen and to his employer. He also speaks English with his wife who is English-medium educated. In spite of his Chinese-medium primary education his speech patterns show definite characteristics of Singapore English (see introduction to this and the previous section).

The text illustrates the changing economic status between two generations of the same family, urbanization in Singapore and the type of taxi known as the 'pick-up taxi'. Pick-up taxis were very popular in Singapore but nowadays taxi drivers charge their passengers according to the meter.

a. About his father

My father came from China; Hailam island. Well, about that time usually all the family try to go other countrie(s) to make some money for the family.[1] They are so poor at that time. Now my father is a bar boy, help in a bar. He was here firs(t) by himself alone, jus(t) like stranger going to an island. Then after some time he make some monéy, he try to bring mý mother over. An(d) then we are born here.

b. Trying to get a flat

For some time I staying in Changi.[2] In kampong,[3] you know. House with atap roof.[4] Now I work, I've been removing out to a flat.[5] I got married, got small son. So hard now to get flat in Singapore. Got to line up, you got to wait for about four, five years. One time, the flat(s) nobody want[6] but government clear the land for new building(s) an(d) so on an(d) so everybody have to go to the flat(s).[7] All of a sudden certain rush to go to the flat(s). So you have to go turn by turn.[8] Even myself waited for two year(s).

c. About taxis

At one time was only Chinese operating the taxi(s)[9] but now the NTUC,[10] you see, taking over. An(d) they pick-up taxi(s)[11] some of them. They're picking up passenger(s) by themselves, don'(t) pay by meter, pay loose.[12] One time, if you are taking taxi, a pick-up taxi from Changi point down to Tanjong Pagar[13] you paid about 80 cen(t)s - whereas if is in a métér[14] - from Changi to Tanjong Pagar you pay abou(t) seven to eigh(t) dollar(s). So a pick-up taxi is more cheaper in Singapóre. But a pick-up taxi you have to share the trip with others. They got two way(s) of doing it whether you go by métér or go by pick-up. You go by meter, you got to pay. From city to Changi you go(t) to pay abou(t) five dollars. Whereas from here cos(t) you abou(t) ten dollars to Changi point.

Notes

1. Usually the younger members of a family left China to find work else-
    where.

2. area at the eastern end of Singapore

3. <u>kampong</u> is originally a Malay word.   In Singapore and Malaysia it
    has come to mean a small village-like settlement usually inhabited
    by Malays or a Chinese dialect group, e.g. Hokkien.   A Chinese
    kampong typically consisted of a number of one-storey houses, a few
    shops and a small temple.

4. with a roof of palm leaf thatch

5. 'Now that I'm working, I've moved to a flat.'

6. 'At one time, nobody wanted flats.'

7. The speaker means that the government redeveloped the land, removed
    kampongs and built highrise flats.

8. 'you have to take your turn'

9. The speaker claims that formerly taxis were owned by Chinese.   This
    is not altogether correct.   There were a number of Indian and Malay
    taxi owners/drivers.

10. NTUC - National Trades Union Congress

11. 'And some of them were/are pick-up taxis.'

12. The speaker means that you pay what the taxi driver asks for or you
    negotiate a price.

13. area near the Singapore Docks

14. 'if you are in a taxi with a meter ...'

TEXT 15

The following text is from a recorded interview with a twenty-five
year old secretary in a small firm.   She has had English-medium education up to Secondary Four and she attended a business course for one year.
Her parents are Hakka.   At home she speaks in Cantonese to her servant,
in Cantonese and Hakka to her parents and mainly in English to her
siblings.   Although the speaker has the same school background as some
of the speakers in earlier texts, she has had more opportunity than some
of them to use English, e.g. at the business college, with her colleagues
at work and with customers.   She also has an English employer.

The text illustrates the use of dialects among Singapore Chinese.
In English-medium schools, Mandarin is one of the compulsory second
languages (see Introduction) but before the recent "Speak Mandarin"
campaign, not much Mandarin was spoken by English-medium educated
Singaporeans.   Hokkien and Cantonese are the most commonly used dialects
in Singapore.   Although there are quite a number of Hakka Chinese in
Singapore and Malaysia, the Hakka dialect is used only as an intra-group
code not a lingua franca within the Chinese community.

About the languages and Chinese dialects she can speak

I: What dialects do you speak at home?

M: I speak Cantonese ah.[1]   My own dialect is Hakka, is <u>Kheh</u>, is the same.
Mandarin, I can speak Mandarin but we don'(t) speak Mandarin at home,
of course.

I: What do you speak at home?

M: Cantonese.

I: Why's that?

M: Because our amah - tha(t) is the domestic help - they're Cantonese
people.   So we converse with thém in Cantonese.[2]   An(d) my own
dialec(t) that is the Kheh.

I: Why do Hakka people refer to themselves as Kheh?

M: Actuallý, because (laugh) I don'(t) know much - but then I thin(k)
is because Kheh is the translation of the word <u>Kè rén</u>[3] in Mandarin.
This like ah, you know, visitor.   Is meant a person going from place
to place.

I: When you go shopping what would you use to the local shopkeepers?

M: Depends ah - what type of péopél they are.   If Chinese - they speak
Hokkien,[4] I will converse with them in Hokkien.   If they're Cantonese
- I spea(k) (laugh) I mean, depends on what type of dialect.

I: You said, you know some Mandarin, did you learn that at school?

M: At school as well as go(t) private tutor at home.

I: You are still learning Mandarin?

M: No - tha(t) was when I was schooling.   I had a private tutor as well
as at school I take.[5]

I: Do you use Mandarin at all in the office?

M: No, 'cause most of the people here can spea(k) English.   Mos(t) of
    them speak English, you see.   Mos(t)ly speak English[6] - seldom in
    Mandarin.   But if they speak to me - I will speak.

I: I like Mandarin.

M: Ya, the Kheh dialec(t) is mixture of Mandarin an(d) Cantonese, you
    know.   Have you heard?[7]

I: Say something to me in Kheh.

M: (Laugh) You find very strange (says something in Kheh) (laughter).
    See is a mixture: Cantonese and Mandarin.

I: Are some of the words the same as in Mandarin?

M: Certain words, certain words, yes.   Are the same.   fàn in Mandarin
    is rice ah.   So we go(t) speak fàn in Kheh.[8]   Eat rice in Mandarin
    is chī fàn but chī is different from the Kheh but fàn in Kheh is the
    same, the same pronunciation.   But (laughter) but I don'(t) speak
    very good Hákká.   I mean the correct Kheh dialec(t).   Ours is all
    mix(ed), you know.   I suppose my paren(ts) not born there - so they
    also speak[9] (laughter).

I: What about Cantonese.   Is your Cantonese different from that spoken
    in Hong Kong?

M: Yes, yes, very much differen(t).   You can tell straigh(t) away they
    are from Hong Kong or from Singapore.   Is different, you know.   If
    you look at the mistakes, you can tell.

Notes

1. ah is used here as an emphatic marker.

2. The speaker's family had only one amah.   The second sentence must be
    taken as a general statement.

3. The speaker appears to mean 'abbreviation'.   The meaning of Kè is
    'guest, visitor' and of rén 'person, people'.

4. 'If they are Hokkien Chinese ...'

5. 'and I also took it (Mandarin) at school.' Note the word order.   The
    emphasized phrase at school is placed before I take.

6. 'I mostly speak English.'

7. 'Have you ever heard Kheh spoken?'

8. 'we also say fàn in Kheh.'

9. The speaker means that her parents were not born in China and that
    they too don't speak what she calls "the correct dialect".

TEXT 16

The following text is from a recorded interview with a forty-six year old Indian (Tamil) sales representative. He has had an English-medium education up to Secondary Four. He speaks Tamil with his wife and English with his children, his friends and at work.

The text illustrates the efforts of the Singapore government to keep Singapore clean. Littering is fined and smoking is prohibited in lifts, on public transport and in cinemas.

About cleanliness and smoking

Singapore more cleaner than J.B.[1] Our Singaporeans here are law abiding citizens. Are also law-fearing citizens - because they be heavily fin(ed). You know, is one of the way(s) of the government tell the people be more cleaner that is.[2] I think the governmen(t) has really ma(de) Singapore - wha(t) shou(ld) I say - minimize dir(t). You see that in the cinemas we cannot have any smoking. We're fine(d) five hund(r)ed dollar(s). An(d) in the lift, in the buses. I'm a smoker myself but for those péopél, non-smokers is a nuisance.[3] I've been trying all my bes(t) to stop this thing but only happen other way roun(d) - I mean - increasing myself.[4] Have no will power. I've seen people stop for few week(s) maybe. They stop only for this period. Then star(t) again. I think something bad happen to me, then I will reform myself.[5]

Notes

1. J.B. = Johore Bharu, a town in Southern Malaysia, just across the causeway from Singapore.

2. The speaker is referring here to the 'Keep Singapore Clean Campaign'.

3. The speaker means "smoking is a nuisance for non-smokers".

4. The speaker means that he is smoking more heavily.

5. 'If something bad happens to me, then I shall stop smoking.'

TEXT 17

The following text is from a recorded interview with a twenty-seven year old clerk in Singapore. She has had English-medium education to Secondary Four and one year at a business college. Both her parents are Cantonese. She speaks Cantonese to her mother, English and Cantonese to her father and her siblings and mainly English at work.

The text illustrates the introduction of the simplified Chinese writing system and of the difference between Hong Kong and Singapore Cantonese.

About Chinese writing

C: The Chine(se) wor(d) is very - I mean very complicáted.[1]
   ðə   tʃaˡni   w3   iz vɛɹi aˡ min vɛɹi kɔmpliketɛd

There's so many stro(ke)[2] bu(t) they now for I mean in
  d̥ɔ̃ɛ·z so mɛni stɹɔʔ   bʌʔ ðɛ: naꟻ fɔ aˡ min ɪn

Singapore those governmen(t) ah ministry they try to shorten
  sɪŋgapɔ d̥ɔ̃oꟻz gʌvənmən a mɪnɪstɹi d̥ɔ̃e· tɹaˡ tə ʃɔtən

those Chinese wor(d).[3] Less stro(ke).[4] For us easier to learn.
  d̥ɔ̃oz tʃaˡniz w3ʔ   lɛs stɹɔʔ   fɔ ʌs iziə tu lɜ:n

Bu(t) for China the exa(ct) wor(d) they don'(t) use tha(t),
  bʌʔ fɔ tʃaˡna ðə eksɛʔ   w3:ʔ   d̥ɔ̃e· doꟻn ju·z ðɛʔ

y'know. They use there the defini(te) Chinese wor(d) they
  jno   ðe juz ðɛ   ðə dɛfɪnɪʔ tʃaˡniz w3·ʔ   d̥ɔ̃e·

don'(t) wan(t) to chan(ge) any Chinese wor(d).[5]
  doꟻ   wʌn   tə tʃeɪn   ɛni tʃaˡniz w3ʔ

I: Is the same Chinese character read differently for different dialects?

C: Ya, for Hong Kong they follow exac(t)ly the Chinese reading.
  ja fɔ hɔŋ kɔŋ d̥e fɔlo eksɛkəli d̥ɔ̃ə tʃaˡniz ɹidɪŋ

Li(ke), you see, today ah li(ke) in Chinese[6] we call jin
  laˡʔ   ju si tudɛ: a laˡʔ   ɪn tʃaˡniz wi kɔl tʃɪn

tia(n), you know, bu(t) in Hong Kong they also say gam ti,[7]
  tjɛ   ju nɔ bʌʔ ɪn hɔŋ kɔŋ d̥ɔ̃e ɔso sɛ: gʌm ti

y'know. Bu(t) we Cantonese in Singapore, we woul(d) call i(t)
  jəno   bʌʔ wi kəntniz ɪn sɪŋgapɔ wi wɔʔ   kɔl ɪʔ

<u>gam yat</u>.   This   is   differen(t).   Sometime   we go   to   Hong   Kong
gʌm jat   d̥ðis   ɪz dɪfɹən   sʌmtaˡm   wi go   tu   hɔŋ   kɔŋ

they   hear   our   diale(ct)   wor(d) - they   know   tha(t)   we   are
ðe   hiə   aˠ   dajəlɛ?   w3ˑ   ðe   no   d̥ðɛ?   wi   a

come   from   other   country.
kʌm   fɹəm   ʌd̥ðə   kʌntɹi

I: You can tell if somebody comes from Hong Kong?

C: Yeah,   can   tell,   can   tell   the   difference.
     jɛə   kɛn   tel   kɛn   tel   d̥ðə   dɪfəɹens

Notes

1. The speaker means that Chinese characters are complicated.

2. 'each character has many strokes'

3. Singapore has now adopted the system of simplified Chinese characters.

4. 'There are fewer strokes' (in the simplified characters).

5. The speaker is under the impression that in the People's Republic of
    China (PRC) they don't use the simplified system but the full
    characters. In fact, the simplified characters are used in the PRC
    but are not used in Taiwan.

6. 'in Mandarin'

7. <u>gam</u> <u>ti</u> - a Cantonese expression for <u>today</u>.

TEXT 18

The following text is from a recorded interview with a twenty-eight year old sales manager. He is English-medium educated up to Secondary Four. Both his parents are Hokkien. He speaks Hokkien to his parents and Hokkien and English to his siblings. He uses English with his wife and children and at work.

Danger in a foreign city

I thin(k) - when I sat in the taxi ah,[1] the taxi-man wind up the window and lo(ck) up the door. I say "Why you do that?" That time I was alone you see - night time lah - evening I went out. He say "Oh, you don'(t) know. Evening time ah - at this place where usually got traffic jam(s) at this place[2] you know. Then robbers if they see you are foreigner, they have pistol(s), you know - here they hold pistol(s) you know. They open the door - they sit beside you an(d) ask you to take out all your money". Wa! - make me more scared you know. Really!! - you know at that time it jus(t) happen to be evening and the sky is getting darker, darker, darker y'know. Oh! I got real worried 'know - so at last I manage to get to my my - to the hotel lah. So in the hotel ah - you wan(t) to go out, you know wha(t) the people say y'know - even the attendan(t)s and all that - the guards down there say "Evening don'(t) go out". We ask them why, y'know. They say the same thing - véŕy dangerous - robberies - ah - gunmen - they will say the same thing. So the European with me - he tol(d) me - He say "Huh! Got danger - I like to go!" I say "Why?" He say "We like to go if suppose we hear there's a danger. We jus(t) like to go and see. We like to experience it!" So I say "Friend, but for me I'm different, you see - danger to some people like me - you take it as an excitement, right? To some people - they dare not go - they take it as fear - but to me I take it as I should take precaution(s) ah I have family behind me" - So I say "I don'(t) wan(t) to venture. You wan(t) you go. I don'(t) wan(t) to go".

Notes

1. ah is used here as an emphatic marker.

2. 'There are usually traffic jams at this place.'

TEXT 19

The following text is from a recorded interview with a thirty-two
year old nurse.   She is English-medium educated up to Secondary Four and
has trained as a nurse in Singapore.   Her parents are Teochew.   She
speaks Teochew to them, English and Teochew to her siblings and to her
friends and mainly English at work.

About a patient

He was once ah - I think he works in XX Hospital before and what he does
is that everytime he has a drink too many - you know when he was drunk -
what I mean is a drink too many mean he was drunk - he will go to the
hospital and he say "Ah! I have angina pain(s).   I have chest pain(s)"
and then he tell the doctor he got to be admitted to the hospital.   He
insist that he has to be admitted and he is entitled to first class, you
know, and start making demands.   If you are a government servant and you
are retired from government servant you don'(t) have to pay - you only
pay less than 1% I think.   An(d) he insist that - you know hé has to be
admitted to first class and no other.   He insist that he must be given
first good treatment because he wor(k) in the XX Hospital before and then
morning comes along - five o'clock in the morning comes along, you know.
Before that he will be pressing the bell every five minutes.   He wants
water, he wants ovaltine.   And you know, you are so busy in the night,
he doesn't care.   He say - well you have to give it to him because he's
a patient.   Towards 6 o'clock in the morning he star(ts) to pack his bag
and he wants to go out.   He wan(t) - to discharge.[1]   He say he got chest
pain(s) and his heart attack.   He has everything but he wants to go out
by that time - you know why?   Because he use the hospital as a hotel.
His wife - his wife chuck him out when he drinks a little bit too many so
he come to the hospital himself, say "Oh!   I have chest pain(s)" so that
the doctor will admit him ... because he complain of chest pain(s).
Anybody who complain of chest pain(s), they have to admit him.   He stays
for the night - towards morning seven o'clock in the morning - "I want to
go home".   He bring his bag.   He say "Whether you like it or not I'm
going home".   So he pack his bag and walk out.   Oh! whenever he has a
drink or two and his wife chuck him out, you know - throw all his clothes
out of the door, he goes to the hospital.   He treat it as a hotel - Oh,
yes, we do get wise about it but you know we can't do anything about it
because he complain of chest pain(s).   As long as you complain of chest
pain(s), we can'(t) drive you away, you see, because you never know one
day he might just drop dead on the corridor because the doctor drove him
out.

Note

1.   'He wants to be discharged.'

TEXT 20

The following text is from a recorded interview with a twenty-nine year old business executive. He has had an English-medium education and passed his G.C.E. 'A levels'. He has a university degree in economics. His parents are Teochew. He speaks English and Teochew with his mother, English with his father, his wife and his siblings. He speaks mainly English at his place of work.

The text illustrates the attitudes to Chinese (Mandarin) which were very common among English-medium educated Singaporeans. The aim of the recent government sponsored "Mandarin Campaign" has been to change this attitude.

Chinese in English-medium schools in the fifties

Chinese was taught then, you know, in school but unfortuna(t)ely -
tʃaˡniz wɔz θɔ:t ðɛn jənɔ in skʋl bʌt ʌnfɔ:tjɔnɛʔli

I use the word unfortuna(t)ely - I spea(k) very little Ch... I
aˡ juz ðə w3·d ʌnfɔ:tjɔniʔli aˡ spi:? vɛɹi lidl tʃ aˡ

spea(k) Teochew, Hokkien, a bit of Cantonese, Malay, bu(t) I
spi· teɔtʃu: hɔkjɛn ə bid ɔf kæntəni·z məle· bʌʔ aˡ

spea(k) very little Mandarin an(d) I don'(t) comprehen(d) very
spi·? vɛɹi lidl mændəɹin æn aˡ don kɔmpɹəhen vɛɹi

much of i(t) either I - is a shame I know but ah it was the
mʌtʃ ɔvi? i:ðə aˡ iz ə ʃeˡm aˡ noᵒ bʌg a ig wɔz ði:

good norm attitude, I thin(k) taken when you - when you are tha(t)
gʋ·d nɔ:m ætitju:d aˡ θiŋ ge:kn wen ju wɛn ju a ðæ?

age. I don't know whether it's one of effec(t)s of colonialism
e:dʒ aˡ dono wɛðə igs wʌn ɔv ifɛks ɔv kəlɔniəlizm

or whether it's effe(ct) of identification with Western education
ɔ wɛðə igs ifɛ? ɔv aˡdɛntifike:ʃn wið wɛstən ɛdjukeʃn

bu(t) Chinese language then was something not - I thin(k), I
bʌ? tʃaˡni:z læŋgwiʒ ðɛn wɔz sʌmðiŋ nɔt aˡ θiŋ aˡ

thin(k) frown(ed) upon is too strong a word - bu(t) i(t) was no(t)
θiŋ fɹaᵒn ʌpɔn iz tu stɹɔŋ ə wəd bʌ? i? wɔz nɔ?

readily accepted, you know. English was the main medium of
ɹɛdili æksɛpɟɛɟ junɔ iŋgliʃ wəz ðə meˡn midiʌm ɔv

instruction   an(d)   Chinese   was   thrown   in.   Ya,   i(t) ... i(t)   is a
inst ɹʌkʃn   æn   t ʃaˡniːz   wɔz   t̪θ ɹoᵒn   in   ja   iʔ   iʔ   iz ə

pity.   I   loo(k)   a(t)   i(t)   because   there   was   no(t)   enough   stress
piɟi   aˡ lo̞ʔ   æʔ   iʔ   bikɔːz   ðɛᵊ   wɔz   nɔʔ   inʌf   st ɹɛːs

made   on   i(t).   Whether   it   was   the   mental   attitude   of   the
med   ɔn   iʔ   weðʒ̃ː   id   wɔz   dᵊ̃iː mɛntl   ætitjuːd   ɔv   ði

studen(t)s,   whether   i(t)   was   the   mental   attitude   of   the
stuːdɛns   weðə   iʔ   wɔz   ɟᵊ̃ə   mɛntl   ætitjuːd   ɔv   ðə

authorities,   whether   it   was   the   mental   attitude   of   the   teachers
ɔθɔɹitiz   weðə   iɟ   wɔz   ðə   mɛntl   ætitjuˑd   ɔv   ðə   tiːtʃəz

or   the   organization   as   such,   you   know,   we   don't   really   know.
ɔˑ   ɟᵊ̃i   ɔːgænaˡzeˑʃn   æz   sʌtʃ   jənoˑ   wi   doˑn   ɹɛli   noˑ

Because   i(t)   was   no(t)   made ... it   was   a   subje(ct) - but   there
bikɔs   iʔ   wɔz   nɔʔ   meˑɟ   iɟ   wɔz   eˡ   sʌbdʒɛˑʔ   bʌt   ðɛᵊ

was   no   compulsion   tha(t)   you   mus(t)   pass   i(t)   too, you know, to
wɔz   no   kɔmpʌlʃn   ðæʔ   ju   mʌs   pʰaːs   iʔ   tu   junɔ   tu

pass   the   whole   exam   whereas   in   our   school   English - if   you   fail
paːs   ði   ho̞ᵒl   ɛksʌm   we ɹæz   in   aᴐᵊ   skᴐl   iŋgliʃ   if   ju   fel

your   English   language,   you've   had   it.   Tha(t)   was   the   end   of   it.
jə   iŋgliʃ   læŋgwitʃ   juv   hæd   iɟ   ðæʔ   wɔz   ðə   ɛn   ɔv   iɟ

You   may   excel   in   all   your   other   ten,   eigh(t)   nine   subje(cts)   but
ju   meˡ   ɛksɛ́ˑl in   ɔl   jɔˑ   ʌðə   tɛn   eˑʔ   naˡn   sʌbdʒɛ   bʌt

if   you   fail   English ...
if   ju   fel   iŋgliʃ

I. SPOKEN ENGLISH

A. Singapore English

Section (c)

21. Receptionist and bellboys

22. Two male clerks in a government office

23. European woman and two sales assistants

The three conversations are typical of those that can be heard in
Singapore. The Singaporean speakers use a number of the features of
basilectal SgE which have been discussed in the General Introduction and
the introduction to section (a).

TEXT 21

The following text is a conversation between a female hotel receptionist and several bellboys.

Chinese girl (behind reception desk) to Malay bellboy: Le(t) me know
when he come - can lah?

Bellboy: Can.   He che(ck) ou(t) tomorrow?

Girl: No(t) tomorrow.   Che(ck) ou(t) nex(t) Monday, I thin(k)

Two other bellboys join them, one a Malay the other one a Chinese.

Chinese (pointing to first bellboy): He sitting here and talking to her
one,[1] isn't it?[2]   (Laughter)

Notes

1. 'He's the one who is always sitting here and talking to her.'

2. isn't it? is one of the two invariant question tags in Singapore
English.   The other one is is it?

TEXT 22

The following text is a conversation between two clerks at a government office.

Male Chinese clerk (on the phone): I mean, you give us a che(que), y'know.   You canno(t) hel(p) ah?   I don'(t) buy you a drin(k)   (laugh).

(turning to an Indian clerk at the next desk)

He canno(t) pay also.

Indian clerk: Better you see him.

Chinese clerk: Better lah (turning to customer)   Yes, can I help you, sir.[1]

Note

1. Note the switch from basilectal Singapore English to a more formal acrolectal English when addressing an outsider.

TEXT 23

The following text is from a conversation between a European woman (E) and two Chinese (Cantonese) female shop assistants (A and K) at lunch in a small restaurant.

About boyfriends and marriage

A: Is usually through introduction.

K: You know, one boy he bring his frien(d), introduce his frien(d) to ús.

E: Ah, yes ...

K: (interrupts, lively) The grou(p) star(t) to grow an(d) ...

A: (interrupts K) an(d) you ge(t) to know more, more an(d) more.

K: (laughs) More an(d) more!   Haha (pointing to A) She go steady, y'know.

E: If the parents are Cantonese, do they like their daughter to marry a Cantonese boy or don't they mind if he's ...

A: (interrupts) Nowadáys, I don'(t) thin(k) so they min(d).[1] Formerly they did.   Older generation, they min(d) chil(d) to ge(t) marrie(d) to their own dialec(t).[2]

E: What happens if a Cantonese girl marries a Hokkien boy?   What do
    their children speak at home?

A: Usuállý, they follow the mother 'cause the mother is the one who
    always with the chil(d) usuállý - but the father go out an(d) work.
    Evening only come back.

E: Hm.

K: Usuállý chil(d) spen(d) more time with the mother.

Notes

1. Note the use of <u>so</u> instead of <u>that</u>.

2. People of the older generation wanted marriage within the same dialect
    group.

I. SPOKEN ENGLISH

B. Malaysian English

When a speaker comes from a major town, this has been mentioned but if a speaker comes from a smaller town or village, only the state has been given.   This is for reasons of anonymity.

Section (a)

24.   Maid servant (Tamil) from Kuala Lumpur: Herself and her language use

25.   Waiter (Hokkien) from Malacca: Himself and his earlier jobs

26.   Receptionist (Cantonese) from Ipoh: Herself, Hokkien and Cantonese and dialect jokes

As mentioned in the General Introduction, the typical basilectal speakers of MalE are slowly disappearing as its functions are dwindling away.   The main speakers of basilectal and lower mesolectal MalE are still those who had had an English-medium education and are, at least in their employment domain, in touch with native speakers of English (e.g. expatriate employees of foreign firms, tourists).   The speakers in texts 24-26 belong to this group of Malaysians.

TEXT 24

The following text is from a recorded interview with a thirty-two year old amah (maid servant) in a private household in Kuala Lumpur. She has had an English-medium primary education, including two extra years (Form Two) which may be considered as post-primary.   Her mother is Indian (Tamil) as was her father (now deceased).   She speaks English, Chinese and Tamil at home and English to her European employers as can be seen from the text.

The text illustrates well the multilingual repertoire of some Malaysians, particularly those who are not ethnically Malay.

Herself and the languages she uses

I: Did you go to primary school?

R: Ya, abou(t) Form Two, I thin(k).   After tha(t) my father pass away. I don'(t) go to secondárý school.

I: What did you do after that?

R: I have to work many European houses.   They very nice to mé.   Some they wan(t) me.   They wan(t) ta(ke) me back.[1]   My mother don'(t) wan(t) me[2] bu(t) I li(ke) to go see the plácés.   But my mother say is too far for me.

I: When you were a child, did you only speak Tamil at home?

R: Often I mix.   Speak Chinese, English and Tamil.   My sister(s), they
   also can spea(k) Chinese.

I: Why's that?   Where did you learn Chinese?

R: Not learn but we have to stay with a neighbour all the time.[3]   So we
   mix from the small with the Chinese.[4]   Then we mix what they talk -
   so we learn a lo(t).   Like[5] they call us to come an(d) play with
   you.[6]   So we mix up.   From small we mix up the Chinese: Hokkien
   an(d) Cantonese.   Cantonese, I can speak.   I can speak Hokkien.
   Now I thin(k)   I learn a bit Mandarin.   I like to learn the Mandarin.

I: When did you start to learn English?

R: English?   I wen(t) to school.   From school I learn.   I use to speak
   to péopél,[7] you see.   Is English school, you know.

I: Did you have to take Malay?

R: Ya, but las(t) time[8] is no(t) Malay.   Las(t) time is no(t) Malay class.
   Is a few.   Is no(t) stric(t) with the Malay.[9]   Bu(t) now I can
   spea(k) Malay.   I spea(k) to péopél li(ke) they spea(k) to me.[10]
   Then I know how to spea(k).   They answer mé.   Question(s) I have to
   answer.   Then jus(t) I learn from thém.

I: What about your mother?   What does she speak?

R: My mother can spea(k) a bi(t) Chinese.   Bu(t) she can understand(d)
   bu(t) she can'(t) very good spea(k).   Bu(t) all she can understan(d)
   wha(t) we say.[11]   All she can bu(t) she can'(t) spea(k) ba(ck).
   She spea(k) ba(ck) in Tamil.   We use to[12] spea(k) Chinese an(d)
   English mos(t).   Tamil we no(t) very much use a(t) home.   'Cause my
   sister(s)   they ta(lk) Chinese with mé.   My brother, he another one
   who can'(t) speak very well.   Well, he say, why don'(t) you ta(lk)
   Tamil to your mother, talking English an(d) Chinese mixed.   Is funny!

I: What do you speak here?   (at her place of employment) Mainly English?

R: Ya - but once I teach English family.   I teach them bi(t) Indian[13]
   an(d) they wan(t) to learn a bi(t).   Can spea(k) to me[14] when I come
   - like "Goo(d) Morning", you see.   They ta(lk) to me an(d) I ta(lk)
   to thém.

I: Can you cook Tamil dishes?

R: Ya, can.   You like Indian cooking?

I: Oh, I like it very much.

R: Oh, is it?   You know, some they don'(t) take curry, bi(t) ho(t).[15]
   Some, they ma(ke) too ho(t).[16]   But I wor(k) in this house,[17]
   they don't like the curry too ho(t).

I: Can you write in Tamil?

R: Ya - can.   Is véry difficul(t).   Is very har(d) to learn.   Learn
   a(t) school.   A(t) Conven(t) School.   They teach you English an(d)
   Tamil.   I can wri(te) Tamil.

I: I was told you sing in the choir at your church.

R: Ya - is Catholic Church.   Sing every Sunday in the choir.

I: Are the hymns in English?

R: English, Tamil.   Morning service, seven.   They have English choir.

Then we have to sing English songs.   An(d) then we have ei(ght)-
thirty mass.   Sing in Tamil.   If English, they wan(t) the English
service.   Sing English song(s).   Sometime, we have to go somewhere
else.   They call us other church.[18]

I: Is it a very big choir?

R: Ya, sixty over.

I: Are the priests at your church local people?

R: Ya, Tamil an(d) Eurasian.

I: No Chinese?

R: Got some are Chinese also, because from other church.[19]   Any
important dignitary come, meet all together, Chinese all that.[20]

Notes

1.   She means that several of her employers, on leaving Malaysia, wanted
to take her back with them to their own countries.

2.   'My mother didn't want me to go.'

3.   The speaker means that she and her siblings were looked after by a
Chinese neighbour.

4.   'Since we were very young, we have mixed with Chinese people.'

5.   'for example'

6.   'and play with them'

7.   She means that she used her English out of school to speak to other
people.

8.   'formerly'

9.   She means that at the time she went to school, Malay lessons were
not compulsory.   There was less emphasis on Malay.

10.   The speaker means that she improved her Malay by speaking with
Malays.

11.   'But she can understand all we say'

12.   use to is used here as the non-past habitual aspect marker, meaning
'we speak Chinese and English most of the time.'

13.   She means that she taught some Tamil to an English family where she
was employed.

14.   'They could use a few words of Tamil when speaking to me.'

15.   'Some don't like curry because it's a bit hot.'

16.   'There are of course some people who make it too hot.'

17.   'My employers in this house ...'

18.   'They invite us to another church.'

19.   'There are Chinese priests at other churches.'

20.   'When an important dignitary comes, we all meet, including the
Chinese.'

TEXT 25

The following text is from a recorded interview with a twenty-three year old waiter at a small restaurant in Malacca. He has had an English-medium primary education including one extra year (Form One) which may be considered as post-primary. Both his parents are Hokkien. He speaks mostly Hokkien at home and Hokkien, English and Malay at work.

Himself and his earlier jobs

I: What did you do after you left school?

S: After I lef(t) school, I stay a(t) home for few mon(th)s or
aftə aˡ lɛf skʊl aˡ stɛ· æ? hom fɔ fju mʌns ɔ

a year then I search for job. I help my mother buy
a j3ə d̪ŏen aˡ s3·tʃ fɔ dʒɔb aˡ hɛlp maˡ mʌd̪ə bai

vegetable an(d) sometime do the washing. Do my own washing,
veʒtəbəl en sʌmtaˡm du d̪ə wɔʃɩŋ du mai oːn wɔʃiŋ

you know. Is very easy to wash. Then I wor(k) as délívéry
juno iz veɹi izi tu wɔʃ d̪ŏen aˡ w3·? ɛz deliveɹi

boy. They jus(t) pay me very low pay. So after tha(t) I
bɔi d̪ŏe dʒʌs pe· mi veɹi lo peː so aftə d̪ŏɛ? aˡ

ge(t) to know péopél. I go(t) job in small restaurant as a
ge? tu no· pipəl aˡ gɔ? dʒɔb ɩn smɔl ɹestɔrã ɛs ə

door boy. So I learn abou(t) customer, how to persuade thém,
dɔ· bɔi so aˡ l3n əbʌʊ? kʌstəmə hʌʊ tə pəswed d̪ŏɛ·m

ta(lk) to thém. Then I got into hotel tha(t) was three
tɔ? tu d̪ŏɛm d̪ŏɛn aˡ gɔ? ɩntu hotel d̪ŏɛ? wɔz θɹi

year ago. I apply mysel(f). Wor(k) there for almos(t) a
j3ə əgo aˡ əplai maisɛl w3? d̪ŏɛə fɔ ɔmos ə

year an(d) I was kick(ed) ou(t) - by misunderstanding.
jɛə ən aˡ wɔz kɩ? ʌʊ? bai mɩsʌndəstendɩŋ

TEXT 26

The following text is from a recorded interview with a twenty-six year old receptionist from Ipoh.   She has had an English-medium education up to Secondary-Three.   Her father is Hokkien and her mother Cantonese. She speaks Hokkien with her father, Cantonese with her mother and Hokkien, Cantonese or English with her siblings.   At work, she uses English, Cantonese, Hokkien and some Malay.

The text illustrates the difficulty experienced by some Malaysians who are ethnically non-Malay but take Malay as a school subject and the fact that different Chinese dialects may be the 'dominant' dialect in different parts of Malaysia and that there are even variations within a particular dialect according to the region where it is spoken.

a. About herself

Actuallý, I am no(t) highly educátéd.   I star(t) schooling a(t) the age of seven.   I wen(t) to governmen(t) school.   English school.   After 6 years, I flo(p) in one of the exam(s) - so my mother, she ask me to go to priva(te) (school).   So I study there for three year(s).   Then I flo(p), especiallý in Malay ah.   I was goo(d) in Malay, especiallý my teacher say so.   For Chinese girl - no(t) easy.   They give mé another chance bu(t) my mother coul(d)n'(t) affor(d).   In Sta(te) schooling, during my time, we have a school fees abou(t) two dollar fifty cen(ts) per mon(th).   I wen(t) to this priva(te) school, you see - cos(t) fifteen dollar(s) per mon(th).

b. About Hokkien and Cantonese

I mix aroun(d) wi(th) the Hokkien people a lo(t), you know.   The people I mix, they mos(t)ly Hokkien.   More or less my mother mos(t)ly spea(k) to me in Cantonese.   I understan(d) Cantonese.   Mos(t)ly, the Chinese from Ipoh spea(k) Cantonese.   K.L. also Cantonese.[1]   Penang people, they spea(k) Hokkien.   An(d) you can notice Penang people, you see. Their Hokkien are differen(t),[2] you see.   You go to K.L., you see two person(s) passing, you hear wha(t) they say,[3] you see, an(d) they spea(k) Hokkien, you know whether they from Penang or from other par(t)s of Malaysia.   Is differen(t) slang.[4]   Bu(t) Penang Hokkien sound much nicer than other kin(d).

c. About jokes

I: Do you think Hokkien jokes are different from Cantonese jokes?

F: Ya, they lots differen(t).   Because is depen(d) on a lo(t) who tal(k).[5]
    If Cantonese jo(ke), is more - is dirty jo(ke), you see.   An(d)
    Hokkien joke differen(t).   Depend on how you take (it).

I: More a double meaning?

F: Ya, ya, doúbél meaning.   If the joke(s), they have doúbél meaning,
    is either you ta(ke) i(t) the clean way or the dirty way.   Jus(t)
    one wor(d), i(t) mean two thing(s).   Same tone bu(t) is the way

you say i(t).[6]

Notes

1. The speaker means that in Kuala Lumpur, the capital of Malaysia, the dominant Chinese dialect is also Cantonese.

2. The Hokkien spoken in Penang has a stronger Malay influence than that spoken in other regions of Malaysia.

3. 'If you go to Kuala Lumpur and you overhear two passers-by...'

4. 'There are different ways of speaking Hokkien.'

5. 'Because it depends a lot on who's talking.'

6. The speaker means that the word with the double meaning has the same tone on it.

I. SPOKEN ENGLISH

B. Malaysian English

Section (b)

27. Factory supervisor (Hokkien) from Johor: Her work
28. Fashion designer (Hokkien) from Kuala Lumpur: Designs
29. Secondary school teacher (Malay) from Kelantan: Teaching in Malaysian secondary schools
30. Pharmacist (Tamil) from Selangor: Use of Tamil
31. Science student (Cantonese): Getting accommodation and the use of English and Cantonese

---

Texts 27-31 are examples of mesolectal and acrolectal speech. Texts 27 and 28 are more mesolectal and texts 29 to 31 more acrolectal.

As mentioned in the General Introduction, the number of speakers of MalE (type I) is diminishing and more confined to middle and older age groups who have had an English-medium education and have still some contact with native speakers of English and/or with other speakers of MalE (type I). Typical features of mesolectal and acrolectal MalE are similar to those mentioned in the introduction to spoken SgE section (b).

TEXT 27

The following text is from a recorded interview with a thirty-year old factory supervisor in Johor. She has had an English-medium education to Higher School Certificate. Both her parents are Hokkien. She speaks Hokkien to her parents, Hokkien and English to her siblings and friends and Hokkien, Malay and some English at work.

About her work

A: I'm working in a factory. I'm ah - suppose(d) to loo(k)
aˤm w3kɪŋ   ɪn ə fɛktəɹi   aˤm a   səpoz   tu lɔ?

after line of girls, whereby they wor(k) assembling ah -
aftə   laɪn ʌv g3:lz   wɛ·baɪ   d̪e· w3   əsemblɪŋ ə

produc(t)s.[1] So I learn the thing up and I train these
pɹɔdʌks   so ai l3·n   d̪ə t̪ɪŋ   ʌp ən aˤ tɹen   d̪is

girls up and my job is qui(te) interesting because some
g3ls   ʌp ən maɪ dʒɔb   ɪz kwaɪ?   ɪntɹestɪŋ   bikɔs   sʌm

these girls all the problems you come into human relationship
d̪is   g3ls ɔl ðə   pɹɔbləmz ju   kʌm   ɪntu hjumən ɹileʃənʃɪp

everything. So you fin(d) tha(t) some girls you go(t) to
evɹiθɪŋ   so ju faˤn   ðɛ?   sʌm   g3lz   ju   gɔ?   tu

handle i(t) this way, another girl you go(t) to handle
hɛndəl i?   d̪ᵒ̃ɪs wɛ·   ənʌðə   g3·l ju   gɔ?   tu hɛndəl

another way.
ənʌðə   we:

I: How many girls?

A: A(t) presen(t), I'm controlling abou(t) forty-six.
ɛ?   pɹezən   aim kontɹolɪŋ   əbaɷ?   fɔtə sɪks

I: What are your chances in that firm for promotion?

A: As far as we are concern(ed), our salary scale we lo(ck)
ɛs fa ɛs wi a   kəns3·n   awə seləɹi skɛl   wi lɔ?

into it.[2] So we know our maximum. So I thin(k) ah, if I were
ɪntu ɪt   so wi no aɷ mɛksiməm   so ai θiŋ   a   ɪf ai w3

to   stay in   the   firm and   advance mysel(f),   I   still have to
tu   ste·   ιn   d̪ə   f3·m ən   εdvans   maisεl   ai stιl hεv   tu

ta(ke) u(p) another course.   Because ah this factory they
tε?   ʌ?   enʌd̪ŏ̃ə   kɔ·s   bikɔ·s   a   ðιs   fεktɹi   d̪ŏ̃e

are   dealing in   technical things and basically I don'(t) have
a   dilιŋ   ιn   d̪eknikəl   t̪θιŋs   ən   bεsikεli   aˡ don   hεv

a   technical backgroun(d).
ə   teknikəl   bε?gɹaɷn

Notes

1. 'who are assembling the products.'

2. 'We are within a fixed salary scale.'

TEXT 28

The following text is from a recorded interview with a twenty-five
year old fashion designer in Kuala Lumpur.   He has had an English-medium
education up to Higher School Certificate and has done a course in
fashion design.   Both his parents are Hokkien.   At home, he speaks
English to his father and his siblings and Hokkien to his mother.   He
speaks English, Malay and some Cantonese at work.

The speaker had just won a scholarship to do further studies in
England.   He felt that there was a great future for oriental designs in
Western fashions.

Designs

Oríéntal designs are vérý popular.   Becaúse - ís the same with ús.   We
like Wes(t)ern designs because we have seen too much of ours.   Tha(t)
why I feel is grea(t) a(d)vantage for mé, you know, to go study overseas
because I have bés(t) of both wor(lds).   Can ada(pt).   Like kain[1] - you
know in Kelantan.   The men wear narrow type but this - expensive.[2]   Bu(t)
this one by women too - full dress.[3]   Jus(t) yesterdáy, I wen(t) to this
firm.   They ma(ke) special Malaysian design.   I wen(t) there as stúdén(t).
Yesterdáy, I wen(t) to their showróom an(d) they have their cutting rooms
upstair(s).   I as(k) thém[4] an(d) they say you are no(t) allow(ed) to
visi(t) hére.   They afrai(d), I copy ah!   (laugh).

Notes

1. kain is here used for kain songket, a type of material embroidered with gold or silver thread and used as a garment.

2. 'but this type is expensive.'

3. worn as or made into a full dress.

4. The speaker wanted to have a look at their workshop.

TEXT 29

The following text is from a recorded interview with a thirty-two year old secondary school teacher. She is English-medium educated and has passed the Higher School Certificate. After that she attended a Malaysian Teachers College to train as a science teacher for junior secondary schools. Both her parents are Malay. She speaks Malay to them and to her husband, her children and most of her friends. She also uses Malay at school. She uses English only with some of her non-Malay friends.

Teaching in Malaysian schools

S: Secondary school téachérs, they teach from form one to form three. They're college tráined. But íf there are no teachers who are graduate(s), you see, can be recomméndéd[1] to teach form four an(d) five. But the salary is the same. But now, you see, with the implement of the number of graduate(s) coming[2] - so graduates only will teach form four, for(m) five upwards. I(t) depen(ds) on the school. I(f) the school is in rúrál area[3] - there are no graduate(s), you see. So these college train(ed) teachers have to teach form four an(d) form five. The school[4] where I taugh(t) before I came here, there're no graduates yet.

I: Is it very hard to teach in Malaysian schools? I mean, are the children very naughty?

S: You see, I thin(k), is the same case anywhere. For the children, they have differen(t) behaviours, differen(t) standar(d) of achieve-men(t), you see, an(d) differen(t) degree of concentration. So is differen(t). It depen(d)s on théir backgróund, their tradition. So a(t) the school I taugh(t) before I came here, as temporary teacher, I foun(d) - I foun(d) very difficul(t).[5] The clássés - they are naughtý, stupi(d) an(d) stubborn. Bu(t) as children,[6] you see, they can'(t) be tráined - changed by using the hard way, you see. You punish them,[7] you scold them, they hate you more.

I: It often depends on the headmaster, doesn't it?

S: I thin(k), same case in Malaysia also.   For girls school(s) we have
    headmístress - for boys we have headmasters.   I thin(k), the head-
    máster will use more harsh way(s) of discipline an(d) the headmistress
    will use more gentle way(s).   It depends, I thin(k), is also true -
    because if I go to this four schools[8] - I met four differen(t) head-
    máster(s) an(d) headmistress(es) - an(d) the way of organízing the
    school is differen(t).[9]

Notes

1. The speaker means 'they (namely the college trained teachers) can be
    recommended ...'

2. 'with the implementation of a policy to have more graduate teachers.'

3. 'in a rural area.'

4. 'at the school.'

5. 'I found it very difficult.'

6. 'but being children ...'

7. 'if you punish them.'

8. The speaker is referring to the four schools where she had previously
    taught.

9. 'was different.'

TEXT 30

The following text is from a recorded interview with a thirty-two year old pharmacist from Selangor.   She has had an English-medium education and has done a University course at a Malaysian university.   Both her parents are Indian (Tamil) but as they are both English-medium educated, they speak mainly English in the home.   She speaks mainly English with her siblings and Malay and some English at work.

The text illustrates that many English-medium educated Indians in Malaysia, particularly those of a higher socio-economic status, prefer to speak English at home and do not use their Indian language very much.

Language use

I: What languages did you speak when you were young?

R: When I was younger I spo(ke) Tamil a lo(t) because my
    wen aˡ wɔz jaŋgə aˡ spɔʔ tæmɪl ə lɔʔ bɪkɔz maˡ

    paren(t)s began talking to us in Tamil when we were young.
    pɛɹəns bigæn tɔkɪŋ tɵ ʌs ɪn tæmɪl wən wi wə jaŋ

    An(d) then - my neighbours - a lo(t) of them were Malays and my
    ən ðen maˡ nɛːbəz ə lɔʔ əv d̃ᵊem wə məleːz ən maˡ

    - the maid was a Malay - so we also spo(ke) a lo(t) of Malay
    ðə meˡd wəz ə məleː so wi ɔlso spɔʔ ə lɔʔ əv məleː

    - and English.
    ən ɪŋglɪʃ

I: You picked up English before you went to school?

R: Yes - 'cause our paren(t)s spo(ke) English as well as Tamil.
    jɛəs kɔs aᵒ pɛɹəns spɔʔ ɪŋglɪʃ əs wel əs tæmɪl

    But I've forgotten mos(t) of my Tamil.
    bət aˡv fəgɔtən mos ɔv maˡ tæmɪl

I: Do you know any Chinese dialects?

R: Cantonese, a few words here and there. I can understan(d)
    kæntəniːz ə fjuː wɜːds hiˑə ən ðɛᵊ aˡ kən ʌndəstæn

    a lot. I dare no(t) speak it because they've so many
    ə ɹɔt aˡ dɛː nɔʔ spiːk ɪt bɪkɔs ðɛːv so mænɪ

    differen(t) tones - tha(t) you jus(t) spea(k) in the wrong tone,
    dɪfɹən tɔːnz ðæ juː jʌs spiːʔ ɪn ðə ɹɔŋ tɔːn

it means differen(t),[1] you see.   So I can understan(d) bu(t)
ɪt minz dɪfəɹən   jəsi   so aˡ kæn ʌndəstæːn   bʌ?

I daren'(t) ... (laugh)
aˡ dɛˑən

I: Do you use Tamil at all?

R: I am afrai(d), we know little.   Don(t) spea(k) at home.[2] To
     aˡ æm əfɹɛˑ·   wi no lɪtel   dɔn   spi?   æt hɔm   tu

my maid, I have to spea(k) to her.   We have learned[3] lah,
maˡ mɛˡd aˡ hæv tu spi?   tə hɜː   wi hæv lɜˑnt   la

since she came.   Usually, our maids could spea(k) English bu(t)
sɪns ʃi keːm   juʒuliˑ aᵒ mɛˑds kəd   spi?   ɪŋglɪʃ   bʌ?

then this one she couldn'(t).   So in fa(ct) was good for us.
ðen ðɪs wʌn ʃi kədn̩   so ɪn fæ?   wəz gɔd fə ɜs

We learn some more, more to speak.   You have to use the
wi lɜːn səm mɔˑ mɔˑ tu spiˑk   jə hæv tu juːz ðə

language.   Is jus(t), you see, lack of use of the language
læŋgwɪdʒ   ɪs jʌs   je siː lɛkəv   juːs ɔv d̃ðə læŋgwɪdʒ

that you forgotten it.[4]
ðɛ ju fəgɔtən ɪt

Notes

1.   'If you just use the wrong tone it means something different.'
2.   'We don't speak (much) Tamil at home.'
3.   The speaker means that the members of the family had to learn more Tamil.
4.   'If you don't use the language, you'll forget it.'

TEXT 31

The following text is from a recorded interview with a nineteen year
old university student from Kuala Lumpur.   Both her parents are English-
medium educated Cantonese.   Her father is a government official.   She
herself has had an English-medium education up to Higher School Certificate and at the time of the interview was doing a science course at a
Malaysian university.

The text illustrates that sometimes communication problems exist
between members of different Chinese dialect groups, particularly when
children of pre-school age are involved.   It also illustrates what
Malaysian Cantonese feel about their own Cantonese as compared with Hong
Kong Cantonese.

a.   Getting accommodation

I: Are you staying at a student hostel here?

S: Las(t) year I stay(ed) at the hostel here but this year I couldn'(t)
     ge(t) a place.   I'm staying ou(t)side.   I'm renting a room.

I: You have to apply early to get a place in the hostel, do you?

S: Eh, we have to apply - a(t) the beginning of this year - bu(t) the
     number of places available is limitéd.   So - usuallý they give
     preference to firs(t) year studen(t)s an(d) final year studen(t)s.
     I'm in secon(d) year now - so I missed out.

I: Where is the room?   Is it very far from here?

S: No, it's abou(t) one mile away, at X.   Is no(t) very far.

I: Is it all right?

S: Yes,   It ís qui(te) an experience to stay with a fámily.   I'm rent-
     ing a room from a fámily.

I: Is it a Chinese family?

S: Yes - oh (laugh) - but the(re)'s a problem.   Théy spéa(k) Hakka...
     (laugh) ... an(d) I don'(t) understand Hakka.   Bu(t) the paren(t)s
     spea(k) English.   So we converse in English.   An(d) the elder two
     sons are schooling - so they spea(k) English.   But the younges(t)
     daughter is three years ol(d) an(d) no(t) schooling yet.   So she
     speaks Hakka with a bit of Hokkien she picked up here and there and
     one or two words in Cantonese.   So we have - my room mate an(d) I
     have great fun ... (laugh) - speakíng to her (laughter).

I: You are sharing the room with another girl?

S: Yes.

I: Is she Hokkien or ...

S: (interrupts) She's Hokkien bu(t) she is - of course she speaks English
     and she was brough(t) up in Kuala Lumpur - so she speaks Cantonese.
     People in Kuala Lumpur spea(k) Cantonese maínly.

b.   English and Cantonese

I: What do you speak with your sisters, mainly English or mainly
     Cantonese?

S: Well, wé structure the sentence in Cántonese but the key wor(ds)
     will be in English (laughter).

I: Why's that?

S: I don'(t) know - is jus(t) by a habit.   An(d) because of this two
     languages[1] we use - sometimes we use the wróng words in Cantonese
     an(d) usuallý my father would say we have to corre(ct) our language.

I: Because you're mixing two ...

S: (interrupts) Yés, because we're mixing two.   Sometimes it does no(t)
     really mix bu(t) we - we do mix it - an(d) so there is confusion.

I: When you use English words, do you give them a Cantonese tone?

S: No - that's hów we know the difference between a Malaysian and a
     Hongkongese.   The Hongkongese pu(t) the English wor(d)s with Hong
     Kong tone.   So - when we - when I spea(k) to a Hongkongese - I'll
     know at once tha(t) he is from Hong Kong.   Bu(t) when they spea(k)
     Cantonese, their tone is the same as our Cantonese.

I: So you think that your Cantonese is not very different from the Hong
     Kong Cantonese?

S: The pure Cantonese is not differen(t) bu(t) in my Cantonese we have
     a lo(t) of loan words from Malay an(d) from English.   So - there
     many words which the Hongkongese do no(t) understand.

Note

1.   'these two languages.'

I.   SPOKEN ENGLISH

B.   Malaysian English

Section (c)

32.   Waiter (Malay) from Kedah: About himself and different types of
      Malay

33.   School teacher (Malay) from Kelantan: About himself, his parents,
      Kelantan and Kelantan Malay

34 and 35.   Chinese saleswomen at a Penang supermarket: About language
      use

36.   Conversation between a European woman and a Chinese salesgirl

---

   Texts 32 and 33 are of interest as they show the transition from a
type of nativized MalE (similar to SgE) which was developing in Malaysia
to a type of English which is more like an interlanguage spoken by second
or foreign language learners.   The speaker in text 32 has had a Malay-
medium primary education and the speaker in text 33 an all Malay-medium
education but both still have contact with speakers of English, one
through his job in a restaurant, the other one at the university.   It
is noticeable in text 33 that there is a lack of fluency which is not
due to any shyness or diffidence on the speaker's part but simply to his
lack of ability to express himself in English.

   Texts 34 and 35 give a contrast between two saleswomen of approximately the same age, employed at the same supermarket.   One is partly
English-medium educated, the other is entirely Chinese-medium educated.
Most of the answers of the speaker in text 35 cannot be considered as
belonging to nativized MalE but are part of a learner's language.

   Text 36 was included not only for demonstrating the use of one as a
relativizer but also to show some typical sales strategies employed by
Malaysian Chinese.

78

TEXT 32

The following text is from a recorded interview with a twenty-two year old bellboy from Kedah.   He has had a Malay-medium primary education and an English-medium secondary education to Secondary Three.   Both his parents are Malay.   He speaks Malay at home and with his friends and Malay and some English at work.

The text illustrates the language use of a Malay with some English-medium education as well as different regional varieties of Malay and people's attitude to the Malay spoken in Kuala Lumpur.

a.   About himself

H: I wen(t) from Standar(d) One to Standar(d) Six.   I learn Malay school an(d) after tha(t) I wen(t) to English school for three years, for four years.   Because we from Malay school, we have to study one extra year, y'know, for study English.   Then from tha(t) we come to Form One, Form Two, Form Three.   We learn English in primary school in lesson.   Simple English.   Is very simple.

I: You know some Hokkien, don't you?

H: Ya, théy[1] spea(k) to mé.   I can understan(d) bu(t) I don'(t) know how to say.   Because I mee(t) thém all the times.   Some place I wor(k) - This is the secon(d) place I wor(k).   Before[2] I wor(k) in factory.   In factory I speak English mos(t)ly.   Because Chinese there.   Some they don't spea(k) Malay very well.   So I spea(k) - I have to spea(k) English to thém.

b.   About different regional varieties of Malay

You go(t) so many differen(t) type Malays:[3] Pera(k), Ipoh, Kelantan.[4] I mean slang[5] ah.   Mos(t)ly they spea(k) no(t) the same.   Suppose you go to Kelantan or Trengganu[6] they - differen(t) style they spea(k) Malay.[7] But KL side,[8] mos(t)ly they use the boo(k) style.   KL style the bes(t) in speaking Malay.   But sometime in Kedah, Perlis[9] - you come from south[10] you can'(t) understan(d) us spea(k) Malay.   Mean you ta(lk) with us Malay also - very hard to understan(d).[11]   Sometime you come from the rural area, the Malay you spea(k) dífférén(t).   Your diale(ct) is dífférén(t).   So Malay from town area they say: you come from the rural area.

Notes

1. The speaker is referring to his colleagues at work.   He is working at a small Chinese owned hotel.

2. 'previously'

3. 'So many different types of Malay.'   The speaker shows here his insecurity in noun plural marking.   He is not sure which of the two nouns he should mark for plural.

4. Perak and Kelantan are states in Peninsular Malaysia.   Perak is in the West and Kelantan is in the Northeast.   Ipoh is a town in Perak.

5. Many Malaysians and Singaporeans refer to any speech which is some-
    what different from the standard as 'slang'.

6. Kelantan and Trengganu are states in the Northeast of Peninsular
    Malaysia.

7. 'they speak a different type of Malay.'

8. 'but in Kuala Lumpur ...'

9. Kedah and Perlis are Malaysian states. They are both in the North-
    west of Peninsular Malaysia. The speaker himself comes from Kedah.

10. 'If you come from the South ...' The speaker is referring to
    native speakers of Malay from Southern Malaysia.

11. 'I mean, if they (Malays from Southern Malaysia) speak to us in
    their kind of Malay, we find it very hard to understand.'

TEXT 33

The following text is from a recorded interview with a twenty-eight year old teacher from Kelantan who had gone back to the university to do further studies. He has had a Malay-medium primary and secondary education and two years at a teachers' training college. Both his parents are Malay. He speaks Malay at home and to most of his friends. At the university he speaks Malay and some English.

The text illustrates the chances of teachers in Malaysia to upgrade their qualifications and better their status. It also shows that it is now possible for some young Malays from a rural background to obtain professional training at teachers' colleges and universities.

a. About himself

R: My schooling - Malay school.[1] After sekolah menengah[2] I wen(t) to Training Teachers' College.[3] Two years.

I: Why did you want to go back to university?

R: Like this, see. In my school, they are many type of teacher(s). Many degree of teacher(s). Some are graduate, some are jus(t) training teacher(s).[4] When they graduate teacher(s),[5] they ge(t) salary ei(ght) hundred over ah.[6] Bu(t) for us, the training teacher(s), we ge(t) abou(t) - we star(t) abou(t) three ten.[7] So the wor(k) we do as goo(d) ah. Sometime we can do same lah, same wor(k). So we study here.[8]

I: Did you get a scholarship?

R: Well, like this ah. When the schoolteacher, we can come to study.[9] Education depar(t)men(t) give us half pay. Then we have to, after study have to go ba(ck) an(d) teach again.

b. About his family

I: What does your father do?

R: My father is a farmer. Padi planting[10] an(d) vegetable.

I: Does your mother help him?

R: No(t) my mother. They do - we say bertenun kain.[11] Make the sarong[12] ah. Before she sell herself.[13] Now they jus(t) li(ke) the small agent(s) lah. Go an(d) see péopél bertenun kain.[14] Then ta(ke) their kain sarong, then sell them to the other(s).

c. About Kelantan and the Kelantan dialect

I: Why do you like Kelantan?

R: We know Malaysia multi-racial. Kelantan is - the Malays is more there.[15] Then also we can see the Malays there at the marke(t),[16] a(t) the godown[17] there. Is all Malays. The culture of the Malay is still there. Here[18] is mixed. The food also there is more cheap.

I: Is the Kelantan Malay very different from the K.L. Malay?

R: Ya, big differen(ce).

I: In what way?

R: When the words en(d) with n̲.   makan[19] in Kelantan, we call maké
    [make] pergi is 'go'.   We go(t) gi li(ke) tha(t).[20]   Say[21] the
    senten(ce): Where are you going?   In kampung[22] we jus(t) say: Mu
    nak gi mana?[23]   Mu is kamu.

Notes

1. 'I had all my schooling at a Malay-medium school.'

2. 'secondary school'

3. 'Teachers' Training College'

4. 'teachers who went to a teachers' training college'

5. 'When they are graduate teachers ...'

6. 'they get a salary of over eight hundred dollars a month.'

7. 'three hundred and ten dollars'

8. The speaker means that often non-graduate teachers do the same work
    as graduate teachers but at much lower pay.   This is the reason why
    he wishes to upgrade his qualifications.

9. 'When you are a schoolteacher, you can apply for study leave.'

10. The speaker's father is a rice farmer.

11. 'weave cloth'

12. sarong is a piece of cloth worn as a skirt or as a straight dress.

13. The speaker means that his mother used to sell the kain that she
    herself wore.

14. The speaker means that there are now small agents who go around and
    buy from the weavers and then sell the cloth to wholesalers or shops.

15. Kelantan is a state with a predominantly Malay population.

16. The speaker means that most stall holders at markets in Kelantan are
    Malay.   In other parts of Malaysia, e.g. in Kuala Lumpur, there are
    more Chinese or Indian stall holders.

17. 'store'.   godown comes from the Malay word gedung.

18. The speaker means Kuala Lumpur where he is studying at the university.

19. 'to eat.'

20. 'We say gi.'

21. 'Take, for instance, the sentence ...'

22. 'In our village ...'

23. 'You want (to) go where'

24. mu is the shortened form of kamu (you).

TEXT 34

The following text is a recorded interview with a Chinese saleswoman at a Penang supermarket. It illustrates the language use of someone who has had a mixed Chinese-English-medium education.

Language Use

I: Where did you learn your English?

S: A(t) school

I: Did you go to an English-medium school?

S: My secondár̃y is in English school. My primár̃y is in Mandarin school.[1] In Mandarin (school) we learn three language(s): Malay, Mandarin an(d) English. Secondár̃y only one language: Chinese. The res(t) is English. Now the condition(s) change also.[2] Our age - a few years ago (laugh), qui(te) a few year(s) ago, the main subje(ct) is English.

I: Didn't you do any Malay in secondary school?

S: Nowadays, is compulsór̃y subje(ct).[3]

I: Do you speak Malay?

S: Ya, to Malays. An(d) Indians, we spea(k) Malay to thém. Providéd they don'(t) know English. Bu(t) mos(t) of thém, they know Malay.

I: Do you use Mandarin at all?

S: If I spea(k) to those, they don'(t) really understan(d) English, I spea(k) Mandarin.[4]

I: Would you speak Mandarin to Chinese customers?

S: We don'(t) spea(k) straight away.[5] Providéd they spea(k) to ús.[6] Because some of the local Chinese, they English educatéd. No(t) ábél, know, no(t) to spea(k) Mandarin. Try Hokkien firs(t)[7] or English.

I: What are you talking with the others here? Hokkien?

S: Ya, we use to spea(k) Hokkien.[8] Mos(t) of thém (pointing to the other salesgirls) are Chinese educatéd.

Notes

1. 'I went to an English-medium secondary school and to a Chinese-medium primary school.'

2. 'Now the conditions have changed.' Now all government supported secondary education is in Malay.

3. The speaker implies that it was not a compulsory subject in her school-days.

4. The speaker means that she uses Mandarin to those Chinese who don't understand English.

5. She means she doesn't use Mandarin to Chinese customers straight away.

6. She means she waits for the customers to address her in Mandarin.

7. 'I try Hokkien first ...'

8. 'We speak Hokkien.' Note the habitual aspect marker <u>use to</u>.

TEXT 35

The following text is a recorded interview with a Chinese saleswoman at a Penang supermarket. It illustrates the language use of someone who has had a Chinese-medium education.

Language Use

I: What language do you speak at home?

S: Hokkien.   I spea(k) Cantonese also.

I: What do you speak to the customers?

S: Depend(s) on customer.   Sometime we spea(k) Hokkien, sometime we spea(k) Cantonese to thém.   Or Mandarin.

I: What do you speak to Malays?

S: Spea(k) Malay.

I: Where did you learn your English?

S: In Penang.   Schooling time.   Chinese education.

I: You learned English as a second language?

S: Ya.

I: Did you learn Chinese writing?

S: Ya, in kindergarten.   You learn Mandarin writing from kindergarten, you fin(d) i(t) easy.

I: Can you read newspapers in Chinese?

S: Can.   Can write, can read.   (Customer talks to her in Malay.   She replies in Malay, then talks to other saleswoman in Hokkien).

I: Did you have to pass Malay at your school?

S: Ya, ya.   You mus(t) the Malay.[1]   This - Malaysia.[2]
(Customer talks to her in Cantonese.   She replies in Cantonese).

Notes

1. 'You must pass Malay.'

2. 'This is Malaysia.'

TEXT 36

The following text is a conversation in a small dress shop in Kuala Lumpur between a European woman and a Chinese salesgirl.

EW: (looking at one of the blouses on the rack).

SG: You wan(t) this one?

EW: Well, I don't really know ...

SG: (pulls out another blouse) This one nice - really nice. Ten dollar(s) only, chea(p), see.

EW: I think, this one's a bit too frilly. I want to wear it with slacks.

SG: With skir(t) you can - with sla(cks) also. This one, go many style(s) one.

EW: You haven't got anything plainer?

SG: Sorry, don'(t) have.

II. WRITTEN ENGLISH

A. Compositions and notes

Texts 37-46 are impromptu compositions written by Singapore high school students in Secondary One, Secondary Two and Secondary Four (first, second and fourth year in a secondary school).

37. Hakka girl (Secondary One): The birth of a baby

38. Hokkien boy (Secondary One): An old house

39. Hokkien girl (Secondary Two): A Chinese wedding

40. Hakka girl (Secondary Two): A Chinese wedding

41. Hokkien girl (Secondary Four): The end of the race

42. Hokkien boy (Secondary Four): At a provision shop

43. Hokkien boy (Secondary Four): Experiences of a taxi driver

44. Hokkien girl (Secondary Four): A desperate woman

45. Hokkien boy (Secondary Four): Death to an enemy

46. Hakka boy (Secondary Four): A badminton match

Text 47 consists of two telephone messages and Text 48 is an order which was jotted down by a salesgirl.

Naturally, the language used in these compositions varies considerably between the different age groups and even between individual students (particularly in Secondary Four).

Certain characteristic features of SgE which have already been mentioned in the General Introduction and the introduction to IA (Spoken Singapore English) can also be noticed in some of the compositions, e.g. variable marking of noun plural, past tense and 3rd person singular and variable use of definite and indefinite articles and object pronouns. This is particularly noticeable in the compositions of the younger age group (texts 37-40).

Spelling and punctuation of the original scripts have been retained.

TEXT 37

The following text is an impromptu composition by a Chinese (Hakka) girl in Secondary One (first year at secondary school).

Birth of a Baby

When the baby is born we dont celebrete but after a month then there is a celebreshen.   Then the mother is allow to come out.   We Chinese we are different.   After birth we got to stay in the house for 40 days. We cannot come out.   They say that is very bad for health of the lady after birth gos out.   They say the outside air is not good to the body. They got to stay away from the winds and the sun.   Usually now mothers go hospital for birth of baby.   Last time[1] they give birth at home. Now they stay a day or two in hospital.   After that they come home. They are not suppose to tach[2] cold water.   They have to tach all water which has boiled.   They say you tach cold water the air will enter your body.   If cold water there is air.   So after water boil there is no more air.

Most of the mother like boys.   Boy grow big they marry.   Then you gain some wife.   Girl they are being marry and out of the house.   When baby born we Kheh[3] dont say who give the name.   There is discussion among all what the name of the baby.

Notes

1.   'formerly'

2.   'touch'

3.   The speaker means 'we who belong to the Hakka dialect group.'

TEXT 38

The following text is an impromptu composition by a Chinese (Hokkien) boy in Secondary One (first year at secondary school).

An old House

We stay here ten over years already.   Have upstair and downstair. You got diningroom.   Then you got a TV room then a kitchen.   The TV room make into a bedroom.   My mother sleep downstair.   My brother sleep upstair.   And upstair we got three rooms.   One big room.   Cause we are staying with my uncle.   My uncle my fathers brother.   Got two kids, one boy one girl and a wife.   Then there is two room.   One room for my brother that is marry.   The other room for me.   The other sleep downstair where they got TV room.   They can ly there and watch TV.

TEXT 39

The following text is an impromptu composition by a Chinese (Hokkien) girl who is in Secondary Two (second year at secondary school).

A Chinese Wedding

For Chinese when the girl get married a month before the wedding they prepare everything. For girl you got to prepare clothing. When a man marry a wife, the girl got to prepare a lot of new clothing for that. Because the boy parents old people. Some of them dont like if you dont have much clothing, especially jewelery. So you got to buy all this thing beforehand and everything must be new. For the wedding the girl wears white gown. All white. And then you have something on the head. That is usually provided by the boy parents. Here in Singapore the boy will pay the girl money to go and get the clothings. Depends on how much the girl parents have.

My sister marry last year. The day before they marry, the night before my mother would comb the hair for her. Then she mumble something. My sister got to wear all white. White pyjamas. Then she got to sit in front of the alter with josstick[1] to pray. Then my mother comb the hair. Then they say something. I dont know what they say. I think is prayer. Usually that night they wont sleep anymore. Because all the friends they come and chat. Prepare everything for the next day. In the morning they have a makan.[2] Then my sisters friends all come and congratulate her. Then the boy will come at a certain time. The time is been chosen by the boys mother. Depends if twelve o'clock then twelve o'clock sharp he will come. Then my brother will open the door. Then when my brother open the door the boy got to give him red packet where you put money inside. Then he step down go in the room of the house greet my parents. Then my brother must give him a cup of tea to drink when he sit down to wait for my sister to come out. Then again he got to give my brother red packet. After that he go in the room talk to my sister. They come out together. Then he lead her to the car and off they go to their own home. My mother cry. Usually for Asian people the mother would cry. The mother is suppose to put the thing on the head of the daughter. Usually the mother would cry then. Once you put the thing[3] on the head the daughter is consider as outside already. She belong to the husbands family.

Notes

1. 'joss-sticks'

2. 'a meal'

3. 'the traditional head-dress'

TEXT 40

The following text is an impromptu composition by a Chinese (Hakka) girl who is in Secondary Two (second year at secondary school).

A Chinese Wedding

Chinese people sometime they engage before they marry but now they engage marry all together the same time.   So before they get marry they get preparashens.   The bride and the bridegroom hunt for a room.   They get all the furniture first.   Then they make their dresses.   Then you go and buy gold, gold juleries.   If you are richer you buy more.   If you are not rich you buy less.

Different dialects have different way of marriage.   So we are Kheh,[1] the girl must buy pillow, blanket, sewing machine, cupboard.   All this the girl has to buy.   The rest the man buy.

Before the wedding the mother of the bridegroom and the mother of the bride they make an appointment.   They talk over.   So the brides mother ask from the bridegrooms mother the daury.   The daury is money given to the girls side by the boys side.   This also depends wether the boy is rich.   If the boy is rich may be the daury is a lot but if the boy cant afford so much the daury may be little bit less.   But the boy has to pay something.   And the brides mother if the mother is good buy something for the daughter.   Some mother keep it for themself.

According to Chinese custom the girl before they marry they go to ask someone find out for them in the olden books wether both they can get along.   If they can get along.   What time is best time to get marry.   When my sister got marry they read those book.   They say best time for my sister to get marry to my brother in law is 6 o'clock. Early in the morning.   She got to make up before she get marry.   So my sister ask the ~~butishen~~ beutishen to come midnight!   So she got herself beutify!   So after 6 o'clock everything is ready.   She put on her gown, everything, the bridegroom come to take the bride and his best friend, about 10, escort them out.   There are bridesmaid also.   So 6 o'clock sharp they get into the car.   They go to the mans side first, the bridegrooms side.   And they sit down for a while there have a drink chat.   After that is time for them to take photograph to prove that they got marry.   Before they have the photograph they pray.   Then they change rings.   And in the bridegroom house when you have mother in law you got to give them tea as a respect.   Then if the mother in law is rich then you have some gold chains.   If they rich they give you this. If not rich then you have a red packet with money.

Some couples go away for honeymoon but depend on indiviyduals. Some they dont have money so after marry they stay home.

Note

1. The writer means that she belongs to the Hakka dialect group.

TEXT 41

The following text is an impromptu composition by a Chinese (Hokkien) girl in Secondary Four (fourth year at secondary school).

The End of the Race

"You have lost!   I am the winner.   Ha - - - !"

"No!   You're playing trick on me, or else the winner should be me!"

"I will forgive you for talking such nonsenses as you've lost and have something wrong in your mind!   Bye-bye!"

After John, the winner, had said this he ~~walked away~~ left.

"I will take revenge!   I will!".   This was the only idea Dick had in his mind.

He started his action.

Every year in the Silver Valley, there will be a motor-car race. The winner will have one million dollars.

Last year's winner should be Dick but John played trick by giving the crew who repaired Dick's car some money and put something extra in his car.   That is why he had won.   Dick was said and angry as his mother needed this sum of money for operation.   She died eventually for being not money ~~to cure~~ for her operation.

The last few day before this year's motorcar race, something happened to John.   Every night the owls near his house would start crying and the dogs were barking all night.   During the day, there were something very strange happened on him too.   Finding dead cat in his cupboard, chair disappeared and reappeared, ---

At last, the day for motorcar-race had arrived.   The exciting car race had started.   The audience were so excited as the two cars which belonged to John and Dick were running very close from starting till the interval.

John ~~was~~ unsuccessed his old trick as Dick asked his cousin to overhaul his car for him.

After the interval, the race started again.

At the audienc'e 's seats, the loud speaker had reported this exciting race.

"Until now, nuber 14 (John's car) and number 9 (Dick's car) are still being first two cars.   Now they are along the most dangerous road which has many corners to turn.   Oh! no! Number 14 has failing down from the road to the rocky land below the clift.[1]   Oh, My God!   The car was explored.[2]   Number 9 was the first car to reach the finish point!"

On the way home, Dick was very -happy.

"I've take revenge for you, mother.   John, John, you will never expect ~~for~~ me to use your old trick.[3]   This is called an eye for an eye. Ho - - - -!"

Nobody knew about this matter but Dick was mad at last.

Notes

1. 'Number 14 has veered off the road and is falling down on to the
rocky land below the cliff.'

2. 'the car exploded'

3. 'You never expected me to use your old trick'

TEXT 42

The following text is an impromptu composition by a Chinese (Hokkien)
boy in Secondary Four (fourth year at secondary school).

At a provision shop[1]

After swallow mouthful of bread, which is tasteless to me I open
the door of my shop and begin to deal with my business.   After waiting
for some time, there come a fat-old lady.

"Good morning Ah Mm![2]   What do you like to buy?"

"Can you give me one kg of flour, two packets of salt, two rolls of
toilet-paper, half kg of candle[3] ....."

She wants so many things and she speak so fast that I cannot know
what she really wants.

"Wait! wait! One by one please!"   I stopped her.

I take what she has told me to take.

"Give me half kg of red candle.   I want big one"   After I have
weighed the candle, she add "A!   I think I better want big one.
Change for me! change for me!" she add.   I am so angry but I have to
endure as not to loss[4] any customer.   I change for her.[5]

Suddenly, the telephone rings.

"Way![6]   What you want to kao guan?[7]   A bottle of soy sauce and,
two kg of sugar.   Blk 225[8] ......   Oh!   I don't think I can send to
you today.   As you know, you had ~~only~~ ordered only this few things and
I must see whether there is any people live near you had ordered things
so I can send them together.   "Oh!   I am really sorry!   Why don't
you come down and take.[9]   Then I think you can buy another shop.   I am
sorry!   I hate this kind of people as they think people earn a lot from
them.

After lunch, the weather is so hot and I am really very tire.
Usually, I seldom have business after noon.   I always listen to music
or read some magazines and I find it very dull.

After waiting for a long time, there come a women with two children.

"How much is this?"

"Wua![10] You knock people ah![11]   That shop at the corner sells only 80 ¢ per gram[12] and you sells $1 per gram.   You eat people ah.[13]

Ah Suo![14]   I don't believe la!   The ordinary price is 95 ¢ and I just earn you 5 ¢ only.[15]   How can they sell you 80 ¢?[16]

"Then sell me 90 ¢ la!"[17]

"I am sorry!"

"Ok la! Ok la!   Give me two kg.

"A!   You no eye ah![18]   This one bad one you want to give me"

"All right!   All right!"

This is a typical customer I will meet almost every day.   I most repeat what I had said a few times in a day.   So you know how dull to my life is![19]

Notes

1. A provision shop is a type of traditional small grocery shop.   It can still be found in some older areas of Singapore and in some lower income housing estates.

2. Ah Mm - a Hokkien term used to show respect when addressing older women.

3. 'half a kilogram of candles'   In some provision shops, candles are still sold by weight.

4. 'lose'

5. 'I change the candles for her'

6. way [waˡ] - a Cantonese word for 'hullo', also used by other dialect groups

7. kao guan - a Hokkien expression meaning 'to have dealings with some-one'.   The meaning here would be buy.

8. Blk 225 - Block 225.   Buildings in a housing estate are often numbered

9. 'get the goods yourself'

10. wua - an exclamation of surprise

11. 'you're really fleecing the customers'

12. 'sells that item at 80 cents per gram'

13. eat people - a translation of the Hokkien chia lang meaning 'to cheat or swindle people'

14. Ah Suo - used in Hokkien as a term of address for middle-aged women

15. 'I just make a profit of 5 cents'

16. 'How can they sell it to you at 80 cents?'

17. 'Then sell it to me at 90 cents'

18. The customer is speaking: You no eye ah - a translation from Hokkien lu bo bak chu ah meaning 'can't you see?'

19. 'how dull my life is'

TEXT 43

The following text is an impromptu composition by a Chinese (Hokkien) boy in Secondary Four (fourth year at secondary school).

Experiences of a taxi driver

The first thing I do in the beginning of the day is to drive my wife to the market. My wife carries her basket and walks with me to the taxi. I change the taxi-cab 'Not for hire' to the blue "Taxi".[1]

My wife drops[2] at the market. A fat lady waves her hand and shouting at me to wait for her. She carries a basket of fishes and dirty water is dripping onto[3] my taxi. She wants to go to Block 217.

'You fat woman!' I am thinking and blaming her for giving me to have a hard time in washing my newly bought car, in my mind I know I should not scold her directly since passengers are always in the right position. She pays me two dollar and is gone.

I bought my taxi since last year. It is air-conditioned and with a radio-telephone. I wash my car everyday.

After picking and dropping passengers, it is about 9.00 am I drives to the market and see my wife standing by the road side. She carries her basket and with two chicken packed up.

'Why you buy these chicken?' I asked.

'You are realy very forgetful. Today is the birthday of Tua Pak Gong.[4] I have bought golden paper[5] and jossisticks[6] too' she answered.

It's half past ten! Mrs. Ong should have been waiting for me. Every day I go and picked her up like a private driver. I drive to the detached-house at Serangoon Garden. She smiles at me when we see each other. She is an old lady.

'Where you want to go today?' I said.

'Toa Payoh, Block 77. Ah Tan has been calling me to play "Mahjong" with them for times.[7] Actually I am not willing to go. They always play with such a small amount[8] but if I were not to go, they will scold behind me.[9]

The taxi goes smoothly and suddenly a children rushes out. I stops my car and see nothing happen and go ahead once more. This happens to me at least one a day[10] but I never meet a real accident.

We chatted until we reaches Block 77.

'You will sure win today!' I said.

'Yes, that is! I lost yesterday because you did not give me moral support. Remember to do that everyday!' she said.

She paid me ten dollars and is gone.

I am travelling now at Orchard Road. A European stops me. He wants to go to Bukit Timah. I drive him there. He takes out his purse and hands a fifty-dollars note to me. The price shown on the metre is only fifteen dollars. I try ~~give~~ to change thirty-five dollars back to him.[11]

    'That's all right', he said and walks swiftly.

    I appreciate this type of passengers and hence am lingering at Orchard everyday.[12] Some passengers use to count every cent but I hate them.

    It is afternoon now. An old woman with a lady pregnancy wave at me worryingly.

    'Kandang Kerbau Hospital!'[13] Quick!' she says and hesitating outside the door. At last they get in.

    'Help me! My God! I cannot stand it!' crys out the pregnant woman. She struggles and trying to pull anything she ~~could~~ can reach. Hence I tells the older to lock the door.

    Finally, we arrive. The old lady paid me one dollar.

    'Please! Sir! Pay you tommorow!' they leave with the helpless shouts of the pregnancy.[14] Where am I suppose to collect the money?

    After several revolutions of picking and dropping passengers[15] it is about eight o'clock. I have to return for my dinner and rest.

Notes

1. The writer means: the taxi driver changes the sign 'Not for Hire' to a sign 'For Hire'

2. 'gets out'

3. 'into'

4. <u>Tua Pak Gong</u> - A Chinese god

5. <u>golden paper</u> means 'joss paper' which is paper money burnt as an offering to the gods

6. 'joss-sticks'

7. 'Ah Tan has been ringing up several times to ask me to have a game of 'Mahjong' at her place'

8. She meant that the stakes were not very high

9. 'run me down behind my back'

10. 'once a day'

11. 'to give him 35 dollars change'

12. 'I ply my taxi along Orchard Road every day'

13. Kandang Kerbau Hospital is the Singapore Maternity hospital

14. 'pregnant woman'

15. 'After going around a few times picking up and dropping passengers...'

TEXT 44

The following text is an impromptu composition by a Chinese (Hokkien) girl in Secondary Four (fourth year at secondary school).

A Desperate Woman

The night seems to be extremely silent, the dim light of the moon shine into Mary's house. Mary is pouring kerosene over the wall, and the area around the bed. Mary's husband, Tom was sleeping soundly, he was such a handsome, smart young man, but, Mary hated him, her hatred was not arounsed just in a few minutes time. She had been suffering for three years. During this three years,[1] Tom had biten[2] her for hundreds of times, he slapped her, he kicked her, he pull her hair, he did all kinds of terrible things to her because she had become uglist[3] woman in his mind. She ought to be such a pretty, young girl when he married her, however, after that accident she had become a terrible and ugly creature. Her face was full of scares,[4] most of her face had been damaged during that accident during their honeymoon.

After Mary had been discharged, Tom attitude toward her had changed, he scolded her with vulgar words, slapped her out of nothing and do all sort of cruel things to her.

Tonight, they had a fight again, after dinner, Tom went for a nap. Mary was crying bitterly because of the pain in her body, Mary was pregnent again, althoug Tom know it but he had purposely kicked her again, he told himself he did not want any child, he was afraid that the child might look like the mother, might just as ugly as the mother. Mary was hurt seriously, she had been pregnent once, both it was the same thing. Tom kicked her and she lose her baby, she needed a baby very much. She was so lonely, she hated Tom deeply, but she also love him, anyway, this time, her hatred was much greater that the love she had for him. She wanted to take revenge. Yes, she told herself, she wanted to take revenge. She poured kerosene around the bed. She wanted to kill him, she used a match-stick to start the fire, she walk out silently locked up the door, she sat on the sofa with the key in her hand, she laughed loudly and crazyly "Ha, Ha, Ha, Ha .... Tom, this is your revenge, you had killed my baby, I hated you, I really hated you, now, I wanted to see that you are burnt completely. Ha, Ha ....." Tom was now wake up by the heat and he was shocked about the thing happening, he shoutd[5] loudly for help, he kicked the door, anyway, before he could massage[6] to escape from the fire, he was burnt to death. Finally Mary was comitted to be guilty about the murder, she was sentensed for fifteen years in the jail.

Notes

1. 'these three years'
2. 'beaten'
3. 'the ugliest'
4. 'scars'

5. 'shouted'
6. 'manage'

TEXT 45

The following text is an impromptu composition by a Chinese (Hokkien) boy in Secondary Four (fourth year at secondary school).

Death to an Enemy

Tim was on board the ship neither going for a vacation nor a pleasure trip, he was there for a special purpose.

It was dinner time and every passenger gathered at the canteen. Tim sat just opposite to the man named Samuel John.   This man's misdeeds and wits had caused Tim to bankrupt.   The way Tim looked at him was filled with anguished pain and hatred.

Sam was carrying a large sum of money with him and this money had caused him worried and restless all the time.   He knew he was being followed by his former boss.

The ship had sailed for three days and three nights and everything was peaceful.   Then, on that night, Tim had eventually taken some actions on his plan.   He was unable to do anything as his victim was wary of him.   In his cabin, Tim pulled the drawer out and slipped a dagger into his jacket and then advanced to Sam's cabin.   But the door was locked, he couldn't force it open as this would bring everyone to the scene.   So the only thing he could do then was to collaborate with the person in charge of the cabins.   At first the person in charge of the cabin refused to be with his partnership but Tim managed to persuade him by giving him many advantages.

Unfortunately, his collaborator didn't have the key to his cabin. But Tim had another plan, that is, to poison his victim.   That would certainly need a waitor to do this job.   But Tim didn't want too many people to be involved in his plan so he told his collaborator Jim, "Here, all -you have to do is pretend you are a waiter, right?"   "Sure" said Jim reluctantly.   Then Tim handed Jim a packet of poison.

During that night, Jim took some poisoned dishes and called on Sam for his supper.   And Sam was died the next day.

TEXT 46

The following text is an impromptu composition by a Chinese (Hakka) boy in Secondary Four (fourth year at secondary school).

A Badminton Match

"With such skill and you dare to participate this tournament! Ha! Ha! Ha!" he laughed at me. This had caused the others who were watching the tournament to laugh too.

I was in Secondary One while he was in Secondary Two at that time. It was during a badminton tournament, I had the worst of luck that I had to play with him. I was humiliated when I lost to him in a straights sets. Since that day, I swore that I will beat him one day.

We were both in Secondary four now as he repeated his secondary three. We had another badminton tournament. After three years that I had been pratising badminton, I had hoped for this day to come. The tournament lasted for a few days, we played in different groups. And finally, we both turned out to be the finalists of this tournament.

The final̸ was held on the afternoon of one ̸f Friday. He was quite surprised that I had fought my way to the final. And finally, we met again after three years in the same badminton court, but this time the situation is different, he ~~will~~ would have no chances of ~~beating~~ winning me in straights sets. The hall was crowded with ~~other~~ students and teachers.

The referee ~~has~~ shouted for the game to start. ~~I was nervous as the~~ The crowded hall and ~~noi~~ the noise had made me nervous. To kept myself calm, I tried to run more to ~~heat~~ warm my body. He was too con- fident in the beginning and I had lead the game into Four to Nil. And now, he got a bit hotten up and soon equalized the score.

We were ~~sweating heav~~ perspiring heavily in the hot stuffy hall. I knew his stamina could not match mine and ~~so~~ I used the prolonging tactics against him. We had a duece in the first game and I beat him with three points ahead. I could tell that he got a big surprise and so as ~~the~~ most of the students.

After a five-minute̸ rest we started the second set. He had start- ed playing his best this time ~~but I put in the same~~ and brought the score to seven to one. I continued with my prolonging tactics and the seven to one score had remained for more that ten ~~minute~~ minutes. I could see his face turning red and he was very exhausted. I ~~never kept him gave~~ didn't give him any time to rest and start catching up the score. From seven to one, I made it to seven to fifteen and I had beaten him in straights sets.

TEXT 47

The following text consists of two telephone messages which were written down by different telephone operators in the same Singapore hotel.

Message 1

Regarding your missing baggages. is found in the S'pore Airport, you can go collect any time.   Thank

M.

Message 2

Miss X call.   She say pls call back as soon as possible.   Is urgent.

N.

TEXT 48

The following text is a telephone order for a special fruit basket which was written down by a Chinese salesgirl in a Singapore hotel.

The text illustrates variable noun plural marking as the person who ordered the basket wanted more than one piece of each variety.

(Name & Address)

     oranges

     apple

     pear ?

     bananas

     grape?

        he pay Monday

II.   WRITTEN ENGLISH

B.   From advertising leaflets, packets and menus in
Singapore and Malaysia

49.   On a packet of barbecued dried pork

50.   Leaflet advertising a fish merchant

51.   Leaflet from a cleaning firm

52.   Advertising card from a firm selling tyres and batteries and
      from a tailor.

53.   Advertising leaflet from a supplier of tropical fish

54.   Advertising leaflet from a coaching college

55.   Leaflet advertising fresh eggs

56.   From the price list of a supermarket

57.   From a menu (Singapore restaurant)

58.   From a menu (Malaysian restaurant)

The texts illustrate the use of some of the characteristic features
of SgE and MalE (see General Introduction and introductions to sections
IA and IB).

For example:

(1)   Variable noun plural marking (e.g. texts 55, 56 and 58)

(2)   Noun plural marking where Standard British English does not
      mark for plural (e.g. texts 50 and 53)

(3)   Non-use of d in past participial constructions (e.g. text 53)

(4)   Use or non-use of prepositions in certain constructions, e.g.
      to offer you with (text 50) to cater all patrons (text 51)

(5)   Use of excessively formal, "bookish" vocabulary (e.g.
      texts 51, 52 and 53)

Some of the texts also illustrate the variable use of capital letters
(e.g. texts 52, 54 and 58).

TEXT 49

The following text is from a packet which contained barbecued dried pork.

NAME

ADDRESS

We specialized in making dried-pork

and pork-sliced.

The taste is very delicious.

Our product is good in quality, flavour

and hygienically packed.

(TEXT IN CHINESE)

IDEAL FOR GIFT

TEXT 50

The following text is from an advertising leaflet distributed to householders by a Singapore fish merchant.

We specialize in distributing of fresh fishes for

household consumptions. Requirement of fishes must

be ordered one day before date of requirement.

The following varieties of fishes are as follows:

(Various types of fish are listed)

We can offer you with other types of fishes in your

daily consumptions which are not included above.

NAME

ADDRESS

TEXT 51

The following text is from an advertising leaflet distributed to householders by a Singapore cleaning firm.

Hi, Tenant

Fell excited that Christmas and New Year Seasons are around the corners! Why not give yourself a good and special annual treat; relax at home and let us send our men to do up your residential cleaning and laundry or dry cleaning. You can safe yoursself the time and sweat over year-end cleaning chores and preserve a more youthful you for the season parties.

You can count on the PROS of engaging us for any kind of service appended below:

    -sealing and waxing plus polishing of floor tiles
    -installation of floor tiles and renovation works
     general cleaning
    -laundry and dry cleaning services

and you can expect tip-top services and satisfactions such as

    -reasonable rates plus service right to your door-step
    -save you time, energy, money, machinery cost & manpower
     problems
    -provision of reliable/responsible and trained person

                    Please call us early for appointment

NAME OF FIRM

TEXT 52

The following text is from two sides of an advertising card sent to householders by a Singapore tyre and battery company and a Singapore tailor.

ALL BRANDS TIRES

Electronic Wheel Balancing to all customers.

Dealers in New Tyres, Sport Rims and Batteries. Treading

and service Winding, Starter and Dynamo.

Also outdoor services.   Prompt and courteous services.

NAME OF FIRM

Our shop utilizes the most exquisite imported materials

as well as specialized tailors to cater all patrons.

And uniform prices are reasonable and patrons are assured

of punctual deliveries.

All enquiries are welcomed.

NAME OF FIRM

TEXT 53

The following text is from two sides of an illustrated advertising leaflet distributed to householders by a breeder of tropical fish and supplier of aquarium equipment.

Side 1

Take advantage of our expertise as a breeder for the past 15 years and who, like to exploit, serve, and also providing good know how technology on survival packaging of fishes for exports mainly from our very own holdings. We are also stockist of rare imported species catering for the needs of the overseas market.

Our Aquatic Plants are being source from - X - one of the biggest and most advance cultivated local nursery. All overseas buyers are welcome.

NAME OF FIRM

Side 2

Latest design on aquarium tanks cater for offices, restaurants, hotels, etc., at very economical cost for an improve atmosphere.

ILLUSTRATION

ILLUSTRATION

Made-to-order aquarium tanks to suit individual interior decoration are welcome.

Special Trade Offer: Variety of Fishes and Installation are free on purchases of tank during the show.

NAME AND ADDRESS OF FIRM

TEXT 54

The following text is from an advertising leaflet of a private
teaching institution.

TEACHING OPPORTUNITIES

If you are keen in teaching, you are cordially invited

to our Educational Institution for interview. Full time

and Part-time teaching posts in Academic Subjects are

available for primary to Pre-U level. Salary will

commensurate with your qualification and experiences.

TEXT 55

The following text is from an advertising leaflet distributed to
householders by a supplier of fresh eggs.

Dear Modern Housewife,

     Here we are to serve you. We supply fresh egg

to you at current market rate; and wish to extend our

service to you. For more information, do not hesitate

to contact Mr. X. (telephone number)

     Looking for to serve you,

     Thank you.

TEXT 56

The following text is from a supermarket price list (late 1980). The prices quoted are in Singapore dollars.

SPECIAL OFFER

KELLOFS RICE BUBBLE	250g	2.20
BRILLO PAD	10' S	1.50
SWEETHEART LIME DISHWASHING	32 oz	2.35
RALPHS FACIAL TISSUE U.S.A.	200 X 2 ply	1.70

$$$$$$$$$$$$$$$$$$

AIR-FLOWN ROLLED SIRLOIN	N.Z.	PER/KG	19.50
FRESH GROUND MINCE TOPSIDE	"	"	8.50
FROZEN LAMB NECK CHOPS	"	"	4.20
" LAMB LEGS	"	"	8.60
" HAM STEAK (GAMMON)	HOLLAND	"	11.80

$$$$$$$$$$$$$$$$$$$

TEACHER WHISKY	SCOTLAND	21.95
IRISH MIST IRELAND LEGENDARY LIQUER	IRELAND	13.80
FONOLARI BARDOLINO ITALY REDWINE	ITALY	7.95

$$$$$$$$$$ ORDER NOW ! WHILE STOCK LAST $$$$$$$$$$

TEXT 57

The following text consists of excerpts from a menu of a relatively inexpensive open air restaurant in Singapore.

Our's Speciality:

STEAM BOAT'S

Large $

Small $

B;   B.   Q

BAR - BE - CUE

PORK CHOP	3.50
CHICKEN CHOP	3.50
FISH & CHIPS	3.50
BEEF STICK'S	3.80
CHICKEN WING (5 Stick)	4.00

Try Our's:

COCONUT SPECIAL'S

X COCONUT CREAM $2.80
 (Special's)

COCONUT DRINK'S $1.80

ICE-CREAM'S FLOAT'S

BANANA SPUTS	1.50
PINEAPPLE SPUTS	1.50
SINGAPORE RAINBOW SPECIAL	2.00
SUNDAES COCKTAIL/LOAGAN	1.20
FLOAT'S COKE, 7UP, ORANGE	0.90

HOT/COLD BEVERAGES

COFFEE (for one)	0.80
TEA	0.70
ICE LEMON TEA	0.80
FAESH ORANGE	1.00
FRESH LIME	1.00

SOFT DRINK'S

COKE, 7UP, ORANGE
RT BEER   0.50

CAN DRINK'S

COKE, 7UP, ORANGE
RT BEER   1.00

TEXT 58

The following text consists of excerpts from a menu of a relatively inexpensive restaurant in Malaysia.   No prices are given.

SAVOURIES AND OMELETTE

Fried eggs with chips

Sausages Baked Beans and eggs

Fried Prawn with chips

Plain Omelette

Onion Omelette

ICED CREAM

Plain Iced Cream

Iced Cream with Chocolate Sauce Topping

Iced Cream with Stawberry Sauce Topping

Iced Cream with Lychee

CHINESE DISHES

HOT DISHES

Chicken Chop

Lamb Chop

Pork Chop

Fillet Steak

Fish and chips

SOUP

Pickle Cabbage Soup

Lettuce Soup

Water Cress Soup

VEGETABLE

Fried Sweet Peas

Fried Mixed Vegetable

(Other vegetable can be
  ordered if available)

MEAT

Pork Chop
    (Chinese Style)

Pork Leg with Black
    Mushroom

Beef with Oyster Sauce

Chicken Leg with Black
    Mushroom

II. WRITTEN ENGLISH

C. Newspaper Advertisements and Letters to the Editor

59. Patent medicine

60. Supermarket

61. Supermarket

62. Short advertisements for a masseur, a hairdresser and a dressmaker

63. Two testimonials for a cleansing cream

64. Two short real estate advertisements

65. Excerpts from letters to the editor

As newspaper editors and journalists are extremely conscious of 'standards' and make every effort to come as close to Standard British English as possible, it is not easy to find examples of the typical SgE and MalE in print as even newspaper advertisements and letters to the editor are at times 'vetted' for 'correct' English. There are the occasional features of Sg/MalE in newspaper articles and letters to the editor but as they are relatively scarce and often scattered throughout a lengthy text, it was not considered feasible to include such articles and letters. Only text 65 is a short collection of excerpts from letters to the editor.

TEXT 59

The following text is an advertisement for a patent medicine.

HIGHLY EFFECTIVE

X

Already in the market
    for 15 years

Remedy for 24 types
    of ailments

"Not to worry or fear,
10 minute X can wipe out any
itches-mite affected by
mosquito.   Don't believe?
Try it and follow to
instruction used at No.66"

ILLUSTRATION

TEXT 60

The following is from an advertisement of a small Singapore super-market.   The prices are in Singapore dollars.

SPECIAL		MON - SAT
Whole ·Lychee	565g	1.10
Elbow Macoroni Good food	454g	.80
Marie Biscuit	200g	.70
Mini Bar Mars	250g	2.00
Smarties Milk Chocolate Bean	31g 3 for	1.00
Prawn Cracker Bright Star	40g 2 for	.40

NAME OF SUPERMARKET
ADDRESS

TEXT 61

The following is from an advertisement of a small Malaysian supermarket.

WE OFFER 10% DISCOUNT FOR:

Gent's Dept. = Shirt, T-Shirt, Batek Shirt, Sport Shirt, Neckties, Jackets, Pyjamas, Sweater.

Lady's Dept. = T-Shirt, Blouse, Skirt, Petticoats, Nighties, Jeans, Overcoats, Panties, Brassieres, Girdle, Morning Gown, Beachcoats, Sweater, Swimwear.

Children's Dept. = Dresses, Pyjamas and Babywear.

Leather Goods Dept. = Shoes, Handbags, Belt, Suitcases, Wallet, Purses, Socks, Stocking, Ornaments Cosmetic bags, sandal.

(1 pair of cloth brushes will be given Free for every purchase of one pair of Gent's Shoes)

Textiles Dept., Glassware and Toys Dept.

X FANCY JEANS ARE NOW AVAILABLE FOR SALES IN OUR SUPERMARKET

NAME
ADDRESS

TEXT 62

The following text consists of three short advertisements from a Malaysian daily newspaper.

TIRED?   TENSED?   LET X ...

Agency Provide You with Skilful
Masseuse/Masseur.   Tel. ......
(9.00 onwards)

MADE TO MEASURE ladies'
embroidered Kebaya.   Reasonable
price.   Interested client please
call ......

X   Salong at .....
Tel. ... At your service, facial
bridal make-ups, and latest
scissors cut at $15/-.   Courses
in Hairdressing, Facial and Manicure
available.

TEXT 63

The following text consists of two short testimonials for a
cleansing cream published in a Singapore daily newspaper.

"I had used several expensive face-cleansing products
but all did not have good effect.

A few months ago, I bought X for trial.   Three weeks
later, I am satisfied with it as the pores breathe easily
and my face feels comfortable and has a fragrant smell.

I also use X as night cream and to bathe my baby"

"My husband changed his opinion that I looked like an 'old
lady' and feel that I am still young and lovely.
I will recommend X to the people I know to protect their
faces"

TEXT 64

The following text consists of two short real estate advertisements
in a Malaysian daily newspaper.

Lovely 2 storey detached
house at No. ... Jalan ...
3 Bedroom 2 of which air-
conditioned and a study room -
fully furnished and big garden
together with flower pots.

    Phone ....

Beautiful 2 storey
detached house, 3 bedroom,
bath attached, 1 study,
servant's lovely matured
garden.   Fully furnish.

    Phone ....

TEXT 65

The following text consists of excerpts from letters to the editor
of a Singapore daily newspaper.

NO LAUGHING MATTER

I went back to a polyclinic after having been told that a
molar tooth had to be extracted.
The dentist who attended to me was in fact struggling to have
my tooth pulled out.   During the "struggle", I happened to hold
her hand as I couldn't endure the pain anymore.   Instead of
telling me off nicely, she raised her voice became angry,
apparently at what I did. .... After three days, I noticed
that a portion of the root has not been completely pull out.

ARE THESE PRESERVED FRUITS SAVE?

I would like to know more about the preserved "junk food"
we take in such as ginger slices, plums, etc.
Most of these preserved fruit have rather strong colouring which
stains fingers ...... Most of these packet fruit preserves do
not seem to have any expiry date.   Some of them that I have
bought are spoilt.   If they have expiry date, please show them
on the packets.

A SOLDIER WITH NO PRIDE IS A DISGRACE

It is distressing to see some soldiers getting up buses[1] holding
their berets in their hands.   Some even with their shirts un-
buttoned.   All these can be seen by commuters in the buses.....
Sometimes soldiers conspicuously with their vests tucked out,
are seen crossing the road.
As far as I can recall, I do not remember seeing soldier of
the X Unit which I once served at or the one next to it, doing
any of the sort I have mentioned. .....

Note

1.   'getting on the buses'

TEXT 66

The following text is an excerpt from an article 'The way we speak', published in This Singapore 1975.   Times Publishing Bhd, Singapore.

Language is one of Singapore's many subtleties.   Deceptively western in appearance, apparently speaking English, Singapore traps the unwary westerner into a complacent feeling of being "at home", but in fact, westernisation is only skin deep.   At heart, Singapore is Asian; specifically, Singaporean.

Perhaps a sample Singapore English conversation will illustrate some points.   This is an exaggerated sample of what Ray Tongue would classify as "sub-standard Singapore English" but it serves to underline our point:

A   So, how, man?

B   Can do, lah, mustn't grumble, you know!   You?

A   My daughter's marriage, susa, I tell you!

B   Is it?   Susa, how?

A   Because why, the makan still not ordered up.

B   Alamak!   So late already!   How can?

A   Myself not quite free.   What to do?   Can help or not?

B   Can!

A   You stay close by, isn't it?   Can chit-chat.   I'm having one problem also.   The honeymoon dress is blue in colour but we all don't have to match.   Three hundred-over dollars spent already! Another three hundred, where got?

B   Never mind, lah!   Join me - do you know where is my house?

Here the words "lah", "susa" (trouble), "makan" (food) and "alamak!" (oh dear!) are transferred from the Malay;   structures such as "Can help or not?" come from the Chinese, which poses the positive and negative forms of the verb together to make a question, as in "Can, cannot?" to use a more typical example;   similarly, "can!" is typical of both Chinese and Malay, which repeat the question verb ("Can" in "Can you?") for affirmative replies, instead of using an entirely separate word equivalent to "Yes";   and "Where got?" comes from the Malay "Mana ada?" Tautological structures, such as "Because why" and "Blue in colour", are also typical, as are the use of "Not quite" to mean "Not at all", the use of "We all don't" instead of "Not one of us has", the use of "Stay" for "Live", the use of "Three hundred-over" instead of "More than three hundred" and the structure "Where is my house" instead of "Where my house is".

IV.   ENGLISH IN LITERATURE

A.   Poetry

67. Excerpts from a singapura sequence by Muhammad Haji Salleh

68. Ahmad by Wang Gungwu

69. Excerpt from Big Spender by Ernest Lim

70. Excerpt from Eden 22 by Mervin Mirapuri

As mentioned in the General Introduction, most local writers use a type
of Standard English for their poetry.   Occasionally a few words from
SgE/MalE or from one of the background languages are used in order to
convey a local atmosphere.   The inclusion of typical SgE/MalE speech in
local poetry is rare.   A few examples are given in this section.

TEXT 67

The following text is an excerpt from a singapura sequence by
Muhammad Haji Salleh in The Second Tongue. An Anthology of Poetry
from Malaysia and Singapore, ed. E. Thumboo (1976) Heineman Educational
Books (Asia) Ltd, Singapore. The text illustrates the use of local
lexicon in poetry.

the dawn light absorbs the dust of night
over the sea, and the unwilling sampans[1] tied to bakau poles[2]
are jolted out of broken sleep by silver river waves.
changi[3] grows pale and then blushes gold.
wandering morning breeze sweeps leisurely
along the roads blowing kacang putih[4] containers,
plastic pickled fruit covers to the telephone poles
and fences overgrown with lalang.[5]
it shakes the water surfaces
of laterite puddles.

Notes

1. Chinese type boats.

2. bakau is a Malay word for a type of mangrove. bakau poles
    are mooring poles made from bakau.

3. an area at the eastern end of Singapore island.

4. Malay for 'peanut'.

5. Malay for 'tall, coarse tropical grass'.

TEXT 68

The following text is a poem by Wang Gungwu in <u>The Flowering Tree</u>:
<u>Selected writings from Singapore/Malaysia</u>, ed. E. Thumboo (1970)
Educational Publications Bureau Pte Ltd, Singapore.

The text is an example of Engmalchin - basic English with words from
Chinese and Malay.   This poem is from the early postwar period.

AHMAD

Ahmad was educated.
He never liked his master, but he was.
He can be a clerk, all thought.
But in his heart he had stirrings for Cam,[1]
Where his Head[2] had been, who was so clever.

His wife with child again!
Three times had he fasted,
And puasa[3] was coming round once more.
One hundred[4] to start with - a good scheme;
Quarters, too,
With a room for his two little girls -
Kampong Batu[5] was dirty!

Thoughts of Camford[6] fading,
Contentment creeping in;
Allah has been kind;
Orang puteh[7] has been kind.
Only yesterday his brother said,
Can get lagi satu wife, lah![8]

Ahmad was educated;
The education was complete.

Notes

1. Cambridge University.

2. The British headmaster of the secondary school he had attended.

3. Referring to <u>bulan puasa</u>, the Malay word for the Muslim fasting
    month.

4. One hundred dollars a month.

5. <u>kampong</u> is the Malay word for a village-type settlement.   <u>batu</u> is
    the Malay word for a stone or milestone.   In this case it refers
    to the name for a particular kampong.

6. <u>Cam</u>bridge University and <u>Ox</u>ford University.

7. Malay expression for 'white man' or 'European'.

8. 'You can have another (second) wife'.   <u>lagi satu</u> is a Malay ex-
    pression for 'another', literally 'more one'.

TEXT 69

The following text consists of two excerpts from <u>Big Spender</u> by Ernest Lim in <u>Singapore Writing</u>, ed. Chandran Nair (1977) Woodrose Publications Private Limited, Singapore. They give the atmosphere in a bar through the speech of the bar girl.

...
Come sit next to me,
you won't regret -
I dispense my favours
liberally.
Would you like a drink?
Whiskey, brandy, stout?
Only cost you four dollars,
ten dollars please, my name is Alice,
six for my tip.
....
How about another drink?
 -   Later
Then how about buying me one?
Table 5 one coke,
four dollars please,
you so handsome
 - and you're beautiful
....

TEXT 70

The following text is an excerpt from <u>Eden 22</u> by Mervin Mirapuri
in <u>Singapore Writing</u>, ed. Chandran Nair (1977) Woodrose Publications
Private Limited, Singapore.   The text illustrates how some features
of SgE such as variable use of definite and indefinite articles,
pronoun copying and adjective reduplication can be used effectively
in poetry.

. . . .
i put on
chequered bedspread
many colours
just dried
in tropical sunshine
i put on mongo santamaria
son of preacher man
line up
bill black combo
games people play
place vodka on
side table
in case of thirst
candled dinner
in case of hunger
i send an invitation
come
we dig together
you came
but doorman say
no digging here
your host
he grows beard
his club illegal
but car waiting

to take madam
to cultural festival
with nice
nice person
. . . .

IV. ENGLISH IN LITERATURE

B. Drama

71. Excerpts from <u>A Tiger is Loose in our Community</u> by E. Dorall

72. Excerpts from <u>One Year Back Home</u> by R. Yeo

As mentioned in the General Introduction, there are relatively few
local plays where SgE/MalE is used consistently.   Often some features
of SgE/MalE may be introduced in the speech of some of the characters
but this is often done very haphazardly and does little to contribute
to the whole atmosphere and structure of the play.

However, in the two texts in this section good use is made of
SgE/MalE to aid in character delineation and to establish social and
cultural contrasts between the various characters.

TEXT 71

The following text consists of several excerpts from the play A
Tiger is Loose in our Community by E. Dorall in New Drama One, ed. L.
Fernando (1972) Oxford University Press, Kuala Lumpur.

The play opens in a squatter settlement on the outskirts of Kuala Lumpur.
The characters include 20 year old Chan Choon Hoong, known as 'Tiger',
members of his gang, various other residents of the squatter settlement,
Tiger's 17 year old sister, Helen Chan, Helen's friend Philip Reade, a
Eurasian, Philip's middle-class parents and their amah.

(a) Tiger and the other people of the squatter settlement typically
talk to one another in a basilectal variety of MalE:

PILLAI: What you mean -

TIGER (imitating him): What you mean?   You crook, you lazy slob!   So
                 many days you lie inside there (nodding to his house)
                 snoring and having dirty dreams - what you tell your
                 boss, ah?   Got stomach trouble?   Little toe paining?

PILLAI: If only you know how sick I am -

TIGER: Ah, Tamil story!   You tell it so good.   But - tell
                 me - how much you get paid for sleeping at home, ah?
                 Ten dollar?   Fifteen dollar?   How many times you get
                 sick every month?
                 (No reply.   To SIEW, who is smiling) Hey what you
                 smiling for?   (The smile vanishes from his face.)
                 Think you so good you can laugh at him?

NAGARAJAH: Aiee, Mr. Siew.   We know everything you do.   (He em-
                 phasizes the rhyme.   SWEE SENG and he laugh.
                 NAGARAJAH half chants the following.)   In the little,
                 little flat in Jalan Pasar.

SIEW (gulping): Huh?   What?

NAGARAJAH (laughing): Nemmind lah!   (Puts his finger to his lips.)
                 Top secret, 'The Sexy Afternoons of Mr. Siew.'   Cen-
                 sored for the public.

(b)   In the interlude in the Lake Gardens, Helen's friend Philip uses a
more acrolectal variety than Helen:

PHILIP (quietly):   Helen.

HELEN: Ah?

PHILIP: What's it like - in your home?

HELEN: Ah?   What for you want to know?

PHILIP: Hoong said I know nothing about you really, how you
                    feel and how you live.

HELEN: What you mean, how I live?   Same as other people.

PHILIP: You hardly talk about your mother.

HELEN: I don't see her enough.   My mother works in a
                    coffee shop.   We got a cousin who got a coffee
                    shop, so she work there.   Very long hours, you
                    know.   Sometimes she so tired she sleeps there,
                    don't come home for two or three days.

PHILIP: Then you run the house.

HELEN: Got to.   I come back from school and got to cook
                    and clean up and wash and iron the clothings.
                    Don't ask me, Philip.   I don't want to think about
                    it.

PHILIP: Doesn't Hoong help you?

HELEN: Yes, when he keeps his job.   But always he change.
                    Sometime he fights with them, sometime they fight
                    with him.   Sometime I don't know if he got a job or
                    no.

(c)   Mr. and Mrs. Reade, Philip's parents, speak a more acrolectal type of
English.   The Reade's amah (maid servant) speaks a pidgin-type English.
As mentioned earlier, this type of English is only used by non-English-
medium educated Singaporeans or Malaysians of an older generation who
have regular contact with speakers of English.   In many situations like
the scene below, Bazaar Malay would have been used between an amah and
her employers.   Right at the end of the excerpt, Bazaar Malay is used
between Mr. Reade and the amah.

MR. READE: Hullo.   (He calls out.)   Amah!

PHILIP: Helen, my mother and father.

MRS. READE: Philip has told us a lot about you.

HELEN: I'm - very happy to meet you.

MR. READE: Amah!

AMAH (entering, trying to show to the visitors that she can hold her own
    with her employers):   What?

MR. READE: Here!   (Dumping parcels onto the table.)
                        Take inside.   And orange juice fall down.   Get
                        cloth and wipe, ah?

TIGER: That's all right, I can do it.

MR. READE: It's not necessary.   Amah will do it.

AMAH: Tscha!   I tole Philip she no careful she blake
                        glass.

PHILIP: It's not broken.   The drink only spilt.

AMAH: Huh!   Bloken, spill - I tole her be careful.
                        (Seeing TIGER'S untouched glass on the table.)
                        Tscha!   No even dlink.   (She goes into kitchen
                        with glass and parcels.)

PHILIP: O.K.   It was an accident.

MR. READE: There are some more parcels in the car, Philip.
                        Get them, will you?

PHILIP: Yes, Dad.   (He looks around awkwardly.)   Speak to
                        Helen, Mum.   She's a bit shy.

HELEN (laughing nervously): No lah.

PHILIP: Yes, you are.   You won't say a word if you're not
                        spoken to.

     (He goes out.   The AMAH comes bustling back with a cloth and
        moves towards settee.)

AMAH: Huh!   Where glass?   Ai yah, all the coossin wet.
                        Tscha!

     (She proceeds to mop up.)

MRS. READE: Would you like a drink?

HELEN: No, thank you.   I already had one.   You - you have
                        a very - nice place here.

MRS. READE: Oh.   You like it?

HELEN: Yes.

MRS. READE: I suppose it's all right.   We're looking for a new
                        house though.   This one is a little small for us.

HELEN: Then you should see our house.

MR. READE (to AMAH): Makan siap?[1]

AMAH: Siap![2]

                              Notes

1.   Makan siap? - 'Is the meal ready?'

2.   Siap!   - 'Yes, it's ready.'

TEXT 72

The following text consists of two excerpts from the play <u>One Year Back Home</u> by R. Yeo published in <u>Singa</u> Number 2 (June 1981) published by the Ministry of Culture, Singapore.

The setting is the living room of the Ang's home in Singapore.   Hua, the daughter of Mr. and Mrs. Ang has returned from Europe with her four-year old daughter Lisa.

(a)

HUA: Oh Mee, it's OK lah, I've come back.

MRS. ANG: I know, I know.   (She is still weeping.)

            (She recovers sufficiently to adjust Hua's dress and hair.)

HUA: Stop crying lah, Mee.

MRS. ANG: Why you don't say you were coming back tonight?

HUA: I didn't want to cachow you and pa.

MRS. ANG: What cachow?[1]   We not see you for five years.   If you told us, Sar Che and Sar Ee[2] said go to the airport to fetch you and Li Sa.   Oh, why you don't tell us?

HUA: And Sar Che will come with the uncles and aunties and cousins and make a big fuss at the airport and ask about Lisa.   No thanks, Mee.

MRS. ANG: Oh Hua, why you don't get married?

HUA: Oh Mee, please lah, it's such a long story.   Anyway I didn't want to marry him.

MRS. ANG: But isn't he Li Sa's father?   How can you don't marry the father of your daughter?

HUA: In Europe you can do that.

MRS. ANG: Aiyah,[3] in Europe you can do anything.   Can live together but not marry, can have five, six children and then divorce, can have three or four wives .... I did not want you to go to Europe.   It's all the fault of that boy Richard.   If I see him - where is he now, Hua?

HUA: Richard is now in America.

MRS. ANG: And this man, Li Sa's father.   (She goes to the table, opens a drawer.)   What is his name?

HUA:	Giorgio.
MRS. ANG:	Jojo? (She looks at the photograph of a Caucasian male whose picture she has removed from the drawer.)
HUA:	Gior-gio, not Jojo.
MRS. ANG:	Is this Jojo? (She shows it to Hua who takes it.)
HUA:	Yes, that's him.
MRS. ANG:	(Snatching the picture from Hua and throwing it onto the floor.) Angmo Kwee![4] (Then, abruptly, she turns towards Mr Ang who is still carrying and presumably talking to Lisa. Hua smiles in bemused exasperation.) Li Sa, Li Sa, come Mama pohpoh[5] you. (Carries her.) Mama give you something to eat. (She goes into the kitchen. Mr. Ang goes to talk to Hua.)

(b)

(Mrs. Ang re-enters with Lisa in her arms.)

MRS. ANG:	Li Sa go with Khong Khong. [6] Mama wants to talk to your mother. (She hands Lisa over to Mr. Ang who takes her to the kitchen.) Ah Hua, you want to meet Sim or not? He always ask me when you come back.
HUA:	Who is Sim, Mee?
MRS. ANG:	Aiyah, how can you forget your own cousin? See Khoo's son lah, Sim.
HUA:	(speaking to herself.) Oh him, goodness! O yes Mee, I remember him now. What does he want?
MRS. ANG:	He wants to marry you lah. Even before you go to London, already he asks your Pa and me about you. But you were not interested what. But he still interested. I ask him to come tomorrow, ah Hua?
HUA:	Oh, not so soon Mee. I want to stay at home with you and Pa and telephone some relatives and friends first. Then maybe later Sim can see me.
MRS. ANG:	But he so interested in you? Why you tarek harga?[7] You not married and have a daughter, not many men will want you. Why you be so difficult?
HUA:	Oh Mee, I am interested in getting married but not so soon.
MRS. ANG:	Why not so soon? While you still pretty, better find a husband. Afterwards wait, difficult. And now Sim is a successful businessman, manager of shipyard company in Tanjong Rhu. Very big salary. Ah Hua, you don't have to see him, he will come to see you. I only telephone him and he sure to come. I arrange for him to see you tomorrow, ah Hua?

Notes

1. cachow - disturb

2. 'the third aunt and uncle'

3. an exclamation

4. <u>angmo kwee</u> - 'red-haired devil' used as a derogatory term for a
    Caucasian

5. a Hokkien term meaning 'carry'

6. Hokkien for 'grandfather'

7. 'play hard to get' a Malay expression, literally 'pull the price'

IV. ENGLISH IN LITERATURE

C. Prose

73. Excerpts from Everything's Arranged by Siew Yue Killingley

74. Excerpt from The Taximan's Story by Catherine Lim

75. Excerpt from The Teacher by Catherine Lim

76. Excerpts from A. P. Velloo by Catherine Lim

77. Excerpt from PUB Bills by Ho Khek Fong

78. Little Sister Writes Home by Kirpal Singh

A number of local writers of short stories have included some passages of local SgE/MalE in their works. Usually, however, these are just very brief dialogues or possibly a short speech by one particular person. Exceptions to this are the short story by S. Y. Killingley Everything's Arranged (text 73) and a number of short stories by Catherine Lim (texts 74-76) where the local English has been used with great skill and often subtlety to delineate a particular character or to become itself a protagonist in a struggle between self-expression and correctness (text 75). In the short story PUB Bills by Ho Khek Fong (text 77) SgE dialogue is used throughout the story and the short story by Kirpal Singh Little Sister Writes Home (text 78) is written entirely in Colloquial SgE.

TEXT 73

The following text consists of two excerpts from the short story
Everything's Arranged by Siew Yue Killingley in 22 Malaysian Stories,
ed. L. Fernando (1968) Heinemann Educational Books (Asia) Limited,
Kuala Lumpur.

The main characters are two young Tamil students, Rukumani and her male
friend Devanayagam. They are both at the University of Malaya in Kuala
Lumpur.

(a) The university term is over and the two friends discuss how they
can communicate with each other during the vacation.

Sitting in the lounge, watching the distracting and excited girls
rushing by with packed cases, longing to go home to some decent food,
Rukumani asked Devanayagam, 'This time you think you can write or not?
Can send to Amy's house, what. My mother likes her mother. I can
easily go there to get your letters. But I think better you don't put
my name outside. Can just put 'Miss Amy Wong'. She knows your
writing and won't open.'

'I think so can,' replied Devanayagam, 'but helluva difficult man.
See ah, my sisters brothers all, running all over the house and if I
write they all ask if I'm learning and want to look. Also ah, if I go
to post letter that clerk at the post office can see me. He's a joker,
so sure tell my father I send love letters. But still, try lah!'

Rukumani was a little piqued. It was all right for Deva to be put
off writing to her because he could go out to shows with his friends.
Moreover, he had the tail-end of the vacation to look forward to when he
could come back to the U and not have his family on top of him. She
would have to suffer all sorts of deprivations in Ipoh.

'Suppose you tell them you want to go for shows. Then can simply
go somewhere and just scribble a note to me. Don't think I'm so hard
up ah, but since I suffer for you, at least should write to me when
you're free.'

'Okay, okay lah! Not that I don't want ah, but very difficult.
Also, if you know I love, then should be enough, what; what for want to
write the whole time?'

(b)   On her way home to Ipoh by train, Rukumani meets Johnny Chew, a fellow student, and they talk together.

'So after Finals what you intend to do?'

She asked the current question of their year.

'Oh myself?   Sure fail man,' came the classic answer in an un-convincing tone.

'Eh, don't joke, man.   I think you sure become Assistant Lecturer in the department, if not Lecturer.'

The flattered Johnny was led to reveal his real ambition to become a Sales Representative in one of the big firms.

'Not to say what ah, to become a lecturer is all right.   But think of it ah, now we give them helluva headache;   if myself become one, sure die man.   Sure, sure, got prestige and all, but can't be boddered man. Too much trouble.   Better still become Executive.   Supply and demand, what.   Know that means know everything.   Also ah, you know what I can take if I get fed up?   Can take that what you call Ford pills for Executive Fatigue.   Then also can easily save on big salary, can buy nice Jag and take girl friends for drives.   Can easily tackle and get a good wifie too, but that better not want too soon, because why? Trapped lah!   After, they want this, want that, then worse headache than marking essays, what you think?'

TEXT 74

The following text is an excerpt from a short story The Taximan's
Story by Catherine Lim in Little Ironies - Stories of Singapore (1978)
Heinemann Educational Books (Asia) Ltd, Singapore.

Catherine Lim uses SgE for the whole short story, which is the taxi
driver's part in a dialogue with a lady passenger. The excerpt is the
beginning of the story. Compare it with texts 5 and 8 in Section IA
Spoken SgE.

Very good, Madam. Sure will take you there in plenty good time
for your meeting, madam. This way better, less traffic, less car jams.
Half hour should make it, madam, so not to worry.

What is it you say, madam? Yes, yes, ha, ha, been taximan for
twenty years now, madam. Long time ago, Singapore not like this -
so crowded so busy. Last time more peaceful, not so much taximen, or
so much cars and buses.

Yes, madam, can make a living. So so. What to do. Must work
hard if wants to success in Singapore. People like us, no education,
no capital for business, we must sweat to earn money for wife and
children.

Yes madam, quite big family - eight children, six sons, two
daughters. Big family! Ha! Ha! No good, madam. In those days
where got Family Planning in Singapore? People born many, many
children, every year, one childs. Is no good at all. Today is much
better. Two children, three children, enough, stop. Our government
say stop.

TEXT 75

The following text is an excerpt from a short story The Teacher by Catherine Lim in Little Ironies - Stories of Singapore (1978) Heinemann Educational Books (Asia) Ltd, Singapore.

The story contrasts a schoolgirl's genuine expression of human misery and unhappiness with a teacher's lack of sensitivity and excessive concern for form.

The excerpt is part of the schoolgirl's composition and her teacher's reaction to it.

I was very sad because I don't like to sell cakes I like to learn in school.   But I am scare my father he will beat me if I disobey him so I cannot say anything to him.   He ask me to tell my principal of my school that I am not going to learn anymore. I was scare my principal will ask me questions.   Lucky my mother came home from the hospital where she born the baby, and my mother say to my father that I should learn in school and become nurse later.   So I can earn more money.   Sell cakes not earn so much money.   She begged my father and at last my father agree.   I think he agree because he was in good mood.   If in bad mood like drunk he will beat my mother up and make trouble in the house.   So my mother told me I was no need to stop learning in school.   And that was the happiest day in my life which I shall never forget.

The teacher said slowly and meditatively, "I wonder why most of them write like that?   Day in, day out, we teach grammar and usage.   For my part, I've taught them the use of the Tenses till I'm blue in the face, but they still come up with all kinds of Tense mistakes!   I've drummed into them that when narrating a story or incident, they have to use the Past Tense, but I still get hideous mistakes such as the ones you heard just now."

TEXT 76

The following text consists of two excerpts from a short story
A.P. Velloo by Catherine Lim in _Or Else, the Lightning God and Other_
Stories (1980) Heinemann Educational Books (Asia) Ltd , Singapore.

A. P. Velloo, a retired Indian clerk, finds solace in reading the newspaper and writing letters to the _Straits Times_.

(a)   "'Oil Hike Imminent'."

"These Arabs and Israelis, I tell you, they make trouble for the
world.   Always war, war. Why cannot have peace and men live in brother-
hood?" pondered A.P. Velloo with profound philosophy.

"'By-elections Likely in May'."

"Tchah!   I don't think much of these politicians!" sniffed A.P.
Velloo.

"'Hospital Fees to be Raised'."

"What, what?" exploded A.P. Velloo.   "Hospital fees to go up?
Where got meaning for this?   How can the poor pay high hospital fees?
Where is democratic country if poor suffer all the time?   Tchah!"

A.P. Velloo shuffled out of his flat the better to express his dis-
gust.   The violence, first of the ejection of red betel nut and ceray
juice in an arch to the ground, and second, of the emission forced from
his nose by the pinching of forefinger and thumb, was but a measure of
A.P. Velloo's anger.

"Where got democracy in this country, I ask you?" he demanded, as
he wiped his nose on his shirt sleeve and shuffled back into the flat to
continue reading the paper.

(b)   "Dear Editor Sir,

        Everyday there is crimes in your newspaper.   Young girls
molested in lifts and murder and rape and all sorts of evil things happening.   I should like to know is, What are police doing?   What is
Government doing? How can allow murder and rape and all these things to
go on.   Children they are innocent and precious and we adults must
protect them.   Otherwise our country Singapore whether got tall buildings high rise flats and big grand banks and Courtesy Campaign and
coming by-elections, all this useless without poor people and innocent
children protected from murderers and rapists.   How can say Singapore
democratic country when so much suffering like this?   I beg the Government and all the Police Departments to take action, before situation
gets worst and worst.   We must all strive hard together to make
Singapore democratic country regardless of race or language or religion

creed.   So I hope you will publish my letter in your esteemed newspaper
so all can know of the problem and how problem must be solve by all
faithful citizens.

                              I remain

                              Your Humble

                              Servant

                              A.P. Velloo."

TEXT 77

    The following text is the first part of a short story PUB Bills by
Ho Khek Fong in Singa 3, December, 1981, published by the Ministry of
Culture, Singapore.

The story makes good use of dialogues in SgE to achieve a local
atmosphere.

September, 1980

It was a long and tiring day.   I returned home from work and went to
the wash basin to clean myself.   The landlady came and thrusted a PUB[1]
bill at my face.

    "Eh Mr Ho, don't frighten me!   If every month so much I will die!"[2]

    I fingered the bill.   Eighty-four dollars.   Estimated.

    "Not much what,"[3] I uttered, my face still dripping with water.

    "What not much!   I don't know how you people use water!"[4]

    "Look," I explained, "All your rooms are rented out.   There're
some twelve people in this house, four families.   Average about $7 per
person...."

    She snorted and went away, obviously my simple arithmetic made no
sense to her.

    That night, there was a big commotion in the subtenant, Mr Chan's
room.

    "What!?" I heard his voice above the blaring of his TV set.   "Want
to increase again?"   Last year you already increase us $10, now you
want to increase some more!   Are you all right!?"[5]

"Now everything so expensive...." the landlady retorted.

"Who don't know everything so expensive!   But you already increase last year!"

"That was so long ago.   I also don't intend to increase a lot. Ten, twenty dollars will do."

"Ten, twenty dollars also money, aunty."[6]

"I know.   I try to be reasonable.   Mr Ho just move in last month, I won't increase him."

"Want to increase, everyone increase!"[7] Mr Chan shouted.   "How can you be like that!   Very unfair!   Increase we all, don't increase him![8] Where got reason!"

The landlady mumbled something.

"Okay, Okay-lah.   Want to increase, increase-lah!   Just take it that I eat one chicken less every month!"

Notes

1. PUB = Public Utilities Board, a government body which supplies electricity, gas and water.

2. 'If the bills are always as high as this, it'll be the death of me!'

3. what - a particle which here expresses disagreement and some irritation.

4. 'how you people use so much water'.

5. 'You must be out of your mind!'

6. aunty - an address form used to older women.

7. 'If you want to increase the rent, you have to do it for everyone!'

8. 'You increase our rent but not his!'

TEXT 78

The following text is a short story <u>Little Sister Writes Home</u> by
Kirpal Singh in <u>The Interview and Other Stories</u> (1983) Chopmen Publishers, Singapore.

The story, in the form of a letter, is written entirely in colloquial
Singapore English which provides a good medium for conveying the
intimacy between 'little sister' and 'big sister'.

LITTLE SISTER WRITES HOME

Frangipani
Papua New Guinea

2 November 1982

Aahyaah, big sister, I got something to tell you lah. This place
really fantastic lah. You know, here ah you got to go to court for all
kind of reason lah. You remember the little puppy I told you about or
not? Patchy. This little girl[1] don't know where she find two big
alsation[2] dogs also. Then she bring them home. Aaayah, George and I[3]
really fed up with her. But what to do. Don't know whose dogs also.
But very big you know, and really beautiful. Wah, if in Singapore I
sure to keep them, really nice you know. I took photo to send you -
you look and tell me what you think, okay? But they really give us a
lot of trouble. So terrible. Very funny you know, don't know where
Patchy pick them up from, that girl, aah, really cheeko.[4] We buy very
good food for them you know, so expensive. But they really big and
lovely lah, so no heart to kick them out. We keep them for five days,
still no owner come to claim. Pity our house here no fence lah, or
else we sure to keep them. The owner really funny don't you think?
Leaving two big alsations like that? Good for breeding you know. One
boy, one girl. Still young my neighbour say. But George say too
expensive to keep them. So when nobody come to claim we call the RSPCA
or Doggie Home and ask them come and take these two dogs. But I feel
so bad to send them. But what to do? Cannot keep, wait they bite
people lagi susah.[5] So the dog people come and take them away. But
you know, big sister, here aaah, things really gila[6] lah. Yesterday I
got call from the dog people say I must go to Court and be witness. You
know what happened? Long story, but I cut short for you. Those
Doggie Home, they keep the dogs for one week but no one come to claim,
so you know what they do? They sell the dogs, I still don't know why
they sell, maybe they want funds for the other dogs. Really sad you
know, if you go this Dog House aah, sayang[7] lah, all the dogs and cats
not enough makan,[8] the place also so dirty. So maybe the people think
they sell the alsations, get money and help the Home. But this get

them into plenty trouble.   One month after they sell the dogs, their
old owner came back from holiday.   Don't know what his name, some
orang puteh.[9]   He come back and ask for his dogs back.   But the dog
people say the dogs no more.   Don't know how he find out who got the
dogs.   Wah, he aah, damn daring you know.   One day he go to the new
owner's house and steal the dogs.   So the new owner really fed up boy.
He complain to the dog people who sell him the dogs.   The dog people
also can't do anything.   So they call police.   The police go and ask
the orang puteh give the dogs back.   But the orang puteh don't want to
give them back.   So trouble lah.[10]   Don't know what also.   The new
owner go and sue the old owner for stealing the dogs.   Now become court
case lah.   I also got call in.   I must be witness.   The old owner
say maybe we steal the dogs.   He really kayu[11] you know.   Why we give
the dogs to Dog Home if we steal?   Gila lah that chap.   But I so fed
up with all this.   Do some good thing also you get into trouble.[12]
Terrible.   George very angry you know.   He say to the dog people this
all their business.   Not say he don't want to help the Home,[13] he want,
but he really angry we kena call up[14] go witness in court.   He say the[15]
old owner really mad saying we steal his dogs.   Even Patchy kena fire,
today George come back work he hammer the girl[16] boy, really hammer you
know.   But don't know how now.   Don't know what will happen.   The new
owner sue the old owner for stealing, the old owner sue the Dog Home for
wrongful sale.   And I got to be witness.   Aaayah, not so good lah this
place.   Actually everything good you know, but one little thing like
this sometime can make you fed up.   Can also make you laugh lah.   I
very sad we cannot keep the dogs.   That's why I tell George better
still if we keep the dogs, then no this problem.   But he scared the
dogs bite people lah.   Here ah, if dog bite people you mati[17] boy.
Here got payback system, your dog bite people you pay money or you
kena.[18]   The people come and hantam[19] you.   Sometime they really take
revenge.   Like my neighbour tell me their dog eat other people cat[20] so
he kena pay[21] three hundred dollars, otherwise they want to hammer him
you know.   So George scared lah, but he give excuse say the dogs very
expensive.   Expensive also lah, but we can manage if we plan properly.
Now, see I tell him, for nothing we got problem.   But today lucky the
Dog Home call up say no need to go to court.   They say the old owner
not sure yet.   Also the police if they want me will come and tell me in
writing.   So now I also don't know what to do.   Got to wait and see
lah.   But our Patchy now very good.   She learn to bark already.
Don't know what to do when we come back.   Maybe got to give her to Dog
Home also.   I think the dog people also kheksim with me.[22]   But I got
do nothing wrong what ah, big sister?   Nevermind, I wait and see first.
If anything come up I write again and tell you lah.   Must stop now lah,
got to get makan ready for boss.   Everything okay at home or not?   Say
hullo to everybody okay?   But you don't be scared about[23] this dog
business, maybe it is finished already.   But I tell you only,[24] let you
know this place really funny.   Got all kind of things one.[25]   When the
dog photo ready I send you one.   Everything oright.   Goodbye, write to
me okay?

                                        Little sister

Notes

1. <u>this little girl</u> - refers to the female puppy, Patchy.

2. Alsatian

3. 'I didn't know whose dogs they were either'

4. <u>cheeko</u> - naughty

5. 'We couldn't keep them in case they bit someone and that would've caused a lot of trouble.' <u>lagi susah</u> - Malay for 'more difficult'

6. <u>gila</u> - Malay for 'crazy'

7. 'It's a pitiful sight' <u>sayang</u> - Malay for 'pity'

8. <u>makan</u> - Bazaar Malay for 'food'

9. 'European'. <u>orang puteh</u> - Malay for 'white person'

10. 'What a bother!'

11. 'He's really stupid'. <u>Kayu</u> - Malay for 'wood'

12. 'You do something good and yet you get into trouble'

13. 'It's not that he didn't want to help the Home...'

14. 'we got called up' Kena - used in Bazaar Malay and Baba Malay to form a passive construction

15. 'Even Patchy was roared at...'

16. 'he hit the puppy'

17. 'you've had it!' <u>mati</u> - Malay for 'dead'

18. <u>kena</u> - Malay for 'suffer'

19. <u>hantam</u> - Malay for 'beat up'

20. 'ate somebody else's cat'

21. 'he had to pay'

22. 'I think the people running the Dogs' Home are furious with me'

23. 'don't worry about...'

24. 'I'm just telling you...'

25. 'All sorts of things happen here'

REFERENCES

Bickerton, D. 1975 Dynamics of a Creole System, London: Cambridge University Press.

Chandran Nair (ed.) 1977 Singapore Writing, Singapore: Woodrose Publications.

Crewe, W. (ed.) 1977 The English Language in Singapore, Singapore: Eastern Universities Press.

DeCamp, D. 1971 'Towards a Generative Analysis of a Post-creole Speech Continuum of Languages' in D. Hymes (ed.) Pidginization and Creolization of Languages, London: Cambridge University Press.

Doraisamy, T.R. (ed.) 1969 150 Years of Education in Singapore, Singapore: Publications Board, Teachers' Training College.

Fernando, L. (ed.) 1968 Twenty-two Malaysian Stories, Kuala Lumpur: Heinemann.

_____ (ed.) 1971 New Drama One, Kuala Lumpur: Oxford University Press.

Ho, K.F. 1981 'PUB Bills' in Singa 3/1981, 16-18.

Kirpal Singh 1983 The Interview and Other Stories, Singapore: Chopmen Publishers.

Lim, C. 1978 Little Ironies - Stories of Singapore, Singapore: Heinemann.

_____ 1980 Or Else, the Lightning God and Other Stories, Singapore: Heinemann.

Loh, P. F-S. 1975 Seeds of Separation: Educational Policy in Malaya 1874-1940, Kuala Lumpur: Oxford University Press.

Platt, J.T. 1975 'The Singapore English Speech Continuum' Anthropological Linguistics 17/7, 363-374.

_____ 1977(a) 'The Sub-varieties of Singapore English: Their Sociolectal and Functional Status' in W. Crewe (ed.) The English Language in Singapore, Singapore: Eastern Universities Press.

_____ 1977(b) 'Aspects of Polyglossia and Multilingualism in Malaysia and Singapore' in W.U. Dressler and W. Meid (eds.) Proceedings of the Twelfth International Congress of Linguists Vienna 1977, a special issue of Innsbrucker Beiträge zur Sprachwissenschaft, Institut für Sprachwissenschaft der Universität Innsbruck, 1978.

_____ 1977(c) 'English Past Tense Acquisition by Singaporeans - Implicational Scaling versus Group Averages of Marked Forms' in ITL 38, 63-83.

_____ 1977(d) 'A Model for Polyglossia and Multilingualism with Special Reference to Singapore and Malaysia' in Language in Society 6/3, 361-378.

Platt, J.T.   1978   'Sociolects and their Pedagogical Implications'
RELC Journal 9/1, 28-38.

_____   1979   'Variation and Implicational Relationships: Copula
Realization in Singapore English' _General Linguistics_ 19/1,
1-14.

_____   and Weber, H.   1980   _English in Singapore and Malaysia._
Status: Features: Functions, Kuala Lumpur: Oxford
University Press.

_____   and Weber, H.   1982   'The Position of Two ESL Varieties in
a Tridimensional Model' in _Language Learning and Communi-_
cation 1/1, 73-90.

Ramish, L.   1973   'An Investigation of the Phonological Features of
the English of Singapore and the Relation to the Linguistic
Substrata of Malay, Tamil and Chinese Languages' (Ph.D.
Thesis 1969, Brown University, 1973, Microfilm-Xerox).

Thumboo, E. (ed.)   1970   _The Flowering Tree: Selected Writings from_
Singapore/Malaysia, Singapore: Educational Publications
Bureau.

_____   (ed.)   1976   _The Second Tongue: An Anthology of Poetry_
from Malaysia and Singapore, Singapore: Heinemann.

Yeo, R.   1981   'One Year Back Home' in _Singa_ 2/1981, 84-97.

In the VARIETIES OF ENGLISH AROUND THE WORLD series the following volumes have been published thusfar:

Text Series

T1. TODD, Loreto: *Cameroon*. Heidelberg (Groos), 1982.
     Spoken examples on tape (ca. 56 min.)
T2. HOLM, John: *Central American English*. Heidelberh (Groos), 1982.
     Spoken examples on tape (ca. 90 min.)
T3. MACAFEE, Caroline: *Glasgow*. Amsterdam, 1983.
     Spoken examples on tape (60 min.)
T4. PLATT, John, Heidi WEBER & Mian Lian HO: *Singapore and Malaysia*. Amsterdam, 1983.

General Series

G1. LANHAM, L.W. & C.A. MACDONALD: *The Standard in South African English and its Social History*. Heidelberg (Groos), 1979.
G2. DAY, R.R. (ed.): *ISSUES IN ENGLISH CREOLES: Papers from the 1975 Hawaii Conference*. Heidelberg (Groos), 1980.

Scheduled for 1984:

G3. VIERECK, Wolfgang, Edgar SCHNEIDER & Manfred GÖRLACH (comps.): *A Bibliography of Writings on Varieties of English, 1965-1983*. Amsterdam, 1984.
G4. GÖRLACH, Manfred (ed.): *FOCUS ON: SCOTLAND*.
G5. VIERECK, Wolfgang (ed.): *FOCUS ON: ENGLAND AND WALES*.

- -

VARIETIES OF ENGLISH AROUND THE WORLD is a companion series of books to the journal

ENGLISH WORLD-WIDE
A journal of Varieties of English
ISSN 0172-8865

EDITORS
Manfred Görlach (*University of Heidelberg*)
Braj B. Kachru (*University of Illinois, Urbana*)
Loreto Todd (*University of Leeds*)

From vol. 4, onwards published by John Benjamins Publ. Co.
2 x p/y. ca. 320 pages.

Vol.4. 1983.	Subscr. price	Hfl.	110,--/$	44.00
	Postage	Hfl.	12,--/$	4.80

* Private subscriptions Hfl. 60,--/$ 24.00, postage included (Prepayment required).
Back vols. 1-3 available at current subscription price.